MARK

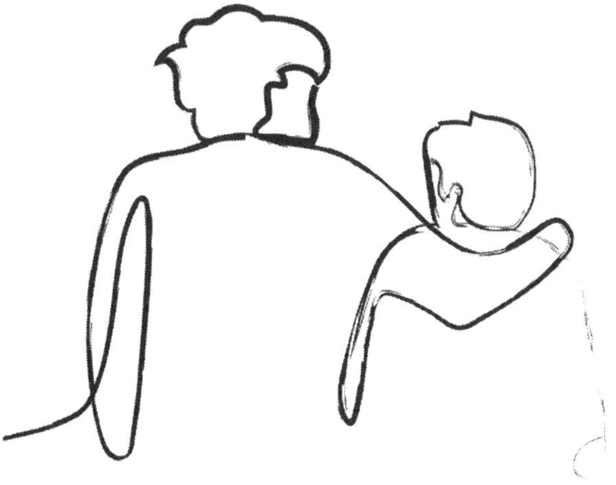

Fathers

The Top 7 Dad Skills

BOOKLAB

First published 2023 by Bella Books UK, a Pawprint/Imprint of BookLab

www.thebooklab.co.uk

British Library Cataloguing in Publication Data A catalogue record for this book is available from the British Library.

ISBN: 978-1-3999-5255-2

Cover design by Esther Kotecha.

Internal illustrations by Daniel Jolliffe.

Printed in the UK

CONTENTS

NOTE FROM THE AUTHOR

This book accompanies the online eight-session eCourse on fathering which is available at www.dad-school.co.uk. Our easy-to-use online course is designed for dads to use at their own pace and in their own time. There are eight sessions on the website. Each one comprises a 25-minute video teaching session given by the Dad School team. There are notes for that session in the accompanying user's manual. We believe this is the most accessible, hands-on, and affordable self-help resource for busy dads today. This volume, *Fathers*, is the official book that participants need to read if they want to go deeper into the content of the eight training sessions on the website.

While this course is grounded in the sciences (especially the science of fatherhood), the ultimate inspiration is a story told by history's most influential teacher, Jesus of Nazareth. This story – wrongly called 'The Parable of the Prodigal Son' – tells the extraordinarily moving tale of a dad who, in terms of his culture, went far further in loving his child than any dad would have been expected to go. Told nearly two thousand years ago, this parable from the world's most charismatic holy man has stood the test of time. There is something eternal and transcendent in its depiction of a father.

You may be a dad who has a religious faith. Or you may be a dad with little or no faith. You may even be a dad who is against religious faith altogether. As you read the pages that follow, you will from time to time run into themes that are spiritual or religious. If you have no faith, or are against faith, we ask a special favour of you, that you would do with this work of nonfiction what you and I do with works of fiction – that is to say, choose to suspend your disbelief for the duration of the journey, if only to benefit from the timeless wisdom within the multi-layered parable that Jesus told.

At Dad School, we as a team believe that this parable should be renamed the Story of a Devoted Dad. For us, it provides a heavenly blueprint for the seven skills that are essential for every father to recognize, cultivate, and perfect in their fathering. Even if you can only interpret this parable as a classic story (i.e., in a literary rather than a faith-related way), that will be enough. May we all learn from the master storyteller how to grow into better dads.

Mark Stibbe, PhD.

THE STORY OF A DEVOTED DAD

There once was a father who had two sons. The younger son did the unthinkable and said, "Dad, I want you to give me what's coming to me after you've died. But I want it now." The father, reeling from this insult, agreed, and divvied out his son's share.

A few days later, the son gathered all his money and possessions and rode out for a far and godless country. There, in an orgy of excessive living, he squandered in a short time everything that his hardworking father had earned over the course of his entire life.

Having lost everything, the boy found himself in even deeper trouble when a recession swept through the land. Along with many others, he began to suffer the dire effects of famine. Desperate times called for desperate measures. The boy approached a farmer.

"I beg you, give me the worst job," he said.

"Very well," the farmer replied. "You can feed the pigs."

The boy winced. Pigs were unclean animals in his religion.

But he had no choice. He was so hungry that he even asked the other workers for some of the pig food. They refused.

Eventually, having hit bottom, the boy had an awakening. Realising that his standard of living was far worse than that of the lowest-paid workers back home, he resolved to return to his father. He prepared a speech in his heart. He would tell his dad that he had sinned against heaven and sinned against him. He would confess that he was not worthy of his father's love - that he would accept being a servant on the farm rather than a son in the house.

Brushing the dirt of the pigpen from his torn clothes, he started the long journey back to his father's house.

Back home, his father had got up that morning thinking that it was going to be another day of grief. He went to the edge of his estate and did what he had done every day and night for several years. He waited at the gates and peered into the distance.

Just then, his fading, ageing eyes detected the silhouette of a man stumbling over the sandy hills of the desert. He recognized the man's demeanour and gait.

It was his long-lost son!

The father was overcome with a visceral feeling of pity. The boy looked so weak, so thin, so forlorn, so desperate.

Lifting his robe above his waist, the father ran as fast as his old legs could carry him towards his boy.

As soon as he reached him, he threw his arms around his son's neck.

He kissed him over and over.

The boy tried to give his prepared confession – the one about sinning against heaven, and so on - but he didn't get more than a few words into it. The father, seeing that some of his servants had caught up with him, had already turned to speak to them.

"Go and fetch the special robe from my house," he cried, interrupting his son's speech. "The one reserved for the most honoured guests who come to our village."

They were about to run back to the house when the father remembered something else.

"Also, bring his ring - the signet ring. You know the one." The servants made to leave again.

But Dad was not done.

"And some shoes. He's a free man, not a slave. So, get him my best leather ones. They'll fit him."

The servants ran back to the father's house and fetched the items. As father and son walked back home – the father supporting his son's thin frame – the servants returned. They put the robe around the boy's shoulders, the ring on his finger, and the shoes on his feet.

As all the villagers turned out to see the return of the prodigal, the father ordered his servants to prepare a great barbeque of prime beef. "Enough for everyone in the village!" he insisted.

As the villagers scratched their heads, he declared, "It's time to have a party! This son of mine was lost, but now he's found. I thought he was dead and buried. But look! He's alive!"

The villagers began to clap, cheer, and dance.

But not everyone was happy.

The father's older son had been working in the fields when he heard joyful music and singing. He asked one of the servants to find out what was going on. When he learned that his younger brother had come home, he shook his head. When he learned that prime beef was roasting on the spit, he began to seethe.

He decided to make it very clear how he felt. He refused to join in with the celebrations.

His father, realising that his older son was unhappy, came out to see him. "Please come and celebrate with us," he pleaded.

"No!"

"Why not?"

"Because it's not fair. All these years, I've been slaving away for you, and not once have you done for me what you've done for him. Not even a roasted goat for me and my mates. Nothing! But when he returns after a wild time wasting all your money on prostitutes, you have an expensive barbeque for the entire village.

How is that right?"

The father sighed and said, "My son. You've always been with me, and everything that you see here has been yours. But this boy has been away for, oh, so long, and he's been destitute. Can't you celebrate too? Can't you be just a little happy that your brother was lost, but now is found … was dead, but now is alive?"

Luke 15:11-32

Author's paraphrase from the original Greek.

DADS ARE WORKS IN PROGRESS

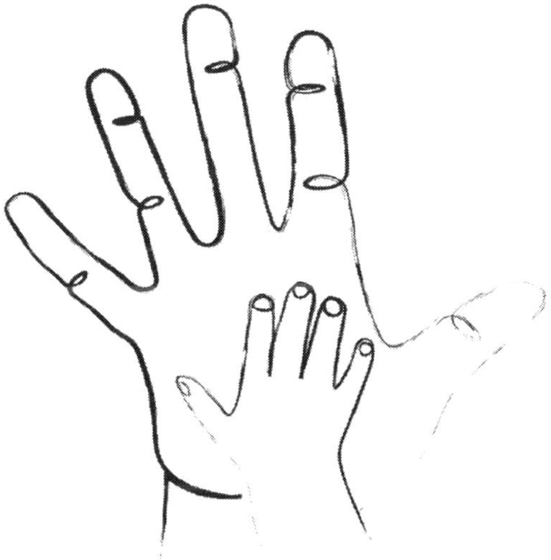

Fathers, like mothers, are not born. Men grow into fathering and fathering is a very important stage in their development.

Dan Gottesman

1
DADS ARE WORKS IN PROGRESS

Maybe you know a father who seems to do everything just right. When they advise their son or daughter, they sound like they're dishing out the wisdom of Solomon. When their children throw a tantrum, they exhibit the patience of Job. When they sing lullabies at bedtime, they display the musical dexterity of King David. When someone threatens the safety of their pack, they stand in the gap and demonstrate the strength of Samson. When their children need empathy, they embody the tearful vulnerability of the prophet Jeremiah. All in all, they appear perfect. And they drive you insane!

If you've seen the film *Jingle All the Way*, you'll know what I'm talking about. Arnold Schwarzenegger plays Howard, a workaholic father. Howard wants to provide for his family, especially his son, Jamie. But, one Christmas, he overdoes it. He's too busy to buy the one toy his son and every other child wants.

The Turbo Man action figure!

When he realises what he's done, Howard's agony is made worse by his neighbour Ted. Ted appears to be the perfect father. He has bought the Turbo Man action figure in good time, knowing full well that the toy is going to be in short supply. He has it already wrapped underneath his Christmas tree. In every way, he masquerades as a better father and man. While Howard fails to make it to his son's nativity play, Ted not only manages to be there for his boy but sits next to Howard's wife flirting with her. Meanwhile, Jamie looks wistfully around the members of the audience for any sign of his dad.

Sound familiar? Maybe you've teetered at the yawning chasm between a seemingly perfect dad nearby and your own imperfect and heart-wrenching attempts.

You've looked in the mirror, seen Howard staring back at you, and realised you've forgotten Turbo Man.

You watch Ted next door - that smiley, well-groomed, ever-loving father who's got his priorities right.

And you hate him.

Almost as much as you hate yourself.

AN ADMIRAL LESSON

As dads, we all have these moments when we feel utterly inadequate. This is normal. Trust me. If we're honest, we all do it from time to time. But the good news is this: it's not just normal, it can also be healthy. While it's possible to overdose on toxic guilt, when we start to engage in healthy realism rather than unhealthy idealism, we are on the way to becoming a better dad.

That's all a bit theoretical, so let me explain.

Have you ever heard of a man called Stockdale?

I mean, *Admiral* Stockdale?

If not, let me introduce him to you. Jim Stockdale became a POW (Prisoner of War) during the long and brutal conflict between South Vietnam and North Vietnam.

The USA supported South Vietnam for most of the twenty-year war, sending tens of thousands of troops to the battle zones. Nearly 60,000 US personnel were killed. Just over 1500 are still missing in action as of March 2023, the time of writing this.

During the Vietnam war, Jim Stockdale became a POW in Hanoi, North Vietnam, after his jet was shot down. At the time, he was the most senior naval officer to be captured. He was routinely tortured in a camp nicknamed the Hanoi Hilton, one of the worst places on earth. During those years, he noticed something about his fellow prisoners. There were some who employed an idealistic perspective, saying, "Our boys are going to rescue us by Christmas." Christmas came, and they hadn't been rescued, so they changed the date to Easter. Then to Thanksgiving. Almost all these guys died of a broken heart. Others embraced a more realistic point of view. They said, "We're in an horrific situation and we're likely to be here some time." These guys, Stockdale observed, tended to survive their ordeal, as Stockdale himself did. He was released after seven years during Operation Homecoming. When asked why he had survived and the idealists hadn't, he said this: "You must never confuse faith that you will prevail in the end - which you can never afford to lose - with the discipline to confront the most brutal facts of your current reality, whatever they might be."[1]

What's the point I'm making here? I'm not suggesting that being a father is anything like being a POW in the Hanoi Hilton, but Jim Stockdale's wisdom does teach dads something. The key to surviving the challenges of fatherhood is not idealism. It's confronting the brutal facts. Be Howard. Don't be Ted.

A HEALTHY DOSE OF REALISM

Let me explain how idealism can be so unhelpful for dads. When we look at the father who seems to have the wisdom of Solomon and the patience of Job, what we often do is we use certain idioms that betray our idealistic and unrealistic notions about fatherhood. We describe that person as "a born father", a "natural father," or as "a gifted dad." Whenever these phrases trot out from our mouths, we reveal the extent to which we've bought into a myth. What is this myth? It's that some fathers are superior because they were either born with an innate ability to father well, or they were somehow gifted by the gods or by God to be a perfect father to their children.[2]

If you believe that, let me tell you something. It's a lie! No one is born a great father. No one is given the *gift* of fathering. All those who are called to become fathers start on an equal playing field. No one is born with some extra ability any more than they are endowed with some mystical capability. The only advantage one father may have over another is the way they themselves were fathered. If someone was fathered well, they will have a greater chance of fathering their own children well. Why? Because they have an example to follow, patterns to copy, practices to emulate. If someone was fathered badly, they miss out on these backstories and blueprints. It's not that they were born with less than someone else, nor is it the case that they missed out on some special heavenly endowment. Rather, they were deprived of the experience of being fathered well, and that's sad.

Becoming a good father is therefore not about genetics or gifting. That's the idealistic view. The realistic view is different. It shifts the focus from genetics and gifting to generations. It says, "we all learn to become good dads over time. If you had a dad who set you a good example, you'll most likely learn more quickly."

So, next time you see a 'Ted', don't be threatened. He's not what you're supposed to aspire to as a dad. He's just someone who's learned to use a few skills well. And, oh yes, one of those skills is not a good skill at all. It's manipulation. He's trying to paint Howard as the worst possible dad so he can seduce Howard's wife. Turns out Ted's not what he pretends to be. Howard's idealistic view is wrong. The real Ted's a nasty piece of work. He's a slimy philanderer.

THE IDEAL FATHER

If people like Ted aren't the ideal for fathers, who is? The answer is found in one of the parables of Jesus.[3] A parable is an ancient Jewish form of storytelling. When Jesus spoke in parables, he told very short stories that contained very big ideas. These stories tended to deal with familiar, earthy realities like people being mugged (the Good Samaritan), farmers out in the fields (the Sower), shepherds in the hills (the Lost Sheep), and employers issuing their employees a workplace challenge (the Talents). In each of these cases, the stories operated at two levels. On the surface, they were cameos of everyday life in first-century Israel. At a deeper level, they were stories that told us something about the kingdom and the culture of heaven.

Take the Parable of the Prodigal Son. You've possibly heard a sermon or two on this story in Luke 15. I can almost guarantee that if you have, it's been all about the younger of the two brothers who does the unthinkable and rebels against his wonderful dad. He heads off to the far country to squander his dad's wealth before having an awakening and coming home. You've probably been told you're like the younger son. You've rebelled by sinning against God's laws. You need to repent and return to God. When you do, you'll be forgiven, just as the prodigal son was forgiven. You'll be saved from your sins and given an invitation to the eternal party in heaven.

Sounds good, doesn't it?

Except that it's a misreading of the story. This story is not about the younger son, or the older son. It's about the most amazing father. He's the kind of father that most of us have been waiting for all our lives. And the good news is this. This dad is a picture of what God our Heavenly Father is like. This is a parable, remember? Parables are down-to-earth fictions that reveal heavenly facts. What's the heavenly fact in this tale? It's that everything you admire in this phenomenal father in Luke 15 is a window onto the father heart of God.

If this is true, then Jesus never meant us to be focused and fixated on the son's sinfulness. He always meant for us to be focused and fixated on the father's exceptional love. So, let's stop dwelling on the younger son and making each other feel guilty. We need to start celebrating the loving father and help people feel grateful. And for those of us who are dads, we also need to see the father in this story as a blueprint for our own fathering. Put bluntly, if you're going to engage in any kind of idealism, then let this dad be your ideal father, not the Teds of this world. The father in Luke 15 sets the bar.

He sets it high.

As high as the heavens.

THE SEVEN SKILLS

Does this mean this dad's example is unreachable? Not at all. One of the main purposes of Dad School is to help people understand that fathering is a matter of learning a set of skills that can be used by everyone, whether they've had a good dad or not. If you lacked a healthy role model in this area, if you missed out on having a good father or father figure, you need to reassure yourself that you have one now. The father in Luke 15 is a portrait of your perfect Heavenly Father. You can learn the skills from him. He invented fatherhood.

What are these skills?

At Dad School, we have identified seven excellent fathering skills the dad uses in Luke 15 and which we believe everyone can use as fathers or father figures. All of us as fathers can use this parable to ask WWDD - what would this dad do?

Firstly, he shows us the skill of fun. The dad in Luke 15 is a fun-loving, party-throwing dad. He loves to celebrate. We can learn from his example about the unique and vital role that comes from the skill of having fun with our children.

Secondly, he shows us the skill of affirmation. The dad in Luke

15 welcomes his son back. He shows that he affirms and accepts him by giving him a robe and a ring. We can learn how vital a dad's affirmation is, and we can learn to use this skill too.

Thirdly, he shows us the skill of time. The dad in Luke 15 gives quality time to both his younger and older sons. He gives them the gifts of his physical presence and emotional engagement. We can learn why this is so vital and excel in this skill too.

Fourthly, he shows us the skill of hugging. The dad in Luke 15 gives his returning, emaciated son the most lavish of hugs. This is a PDA – a public demonstration of affection. This dad hugs the hell out of his son. We can learn to do the same as fathers.

Fifthly, he shows us the skill of setting a good example. This dad provides the most exceptional example to his sons at every level. Setting a good and healthy example to our children is a skill we can learn too as fathers. This dad shows how we can do this.

Sixthly, he shows us the skill of establishing rules. This dad is very loving. We can therefore be sure that he has established love-based not law-based rules. As dads, we can learn some invaluable lessons from this about setting healthy boundaries for our children.

Seventhly, he shows us the skill of security. This dad has spent a lot of time ensuring that he is securely attached to his children, and they to him. Secure attachment is a vital skill. It provides a legacy of good benefits at every level of a child's life.

So, then, here are the seven skills:

F is for FUN
A is for AFFIRMATION
T is for TIME
H is for HUGS
E is for EXAMPLE
R is for RULES
S is for SECURITY

I'm not suggesting that this is the exhaustive, comprehensive, and final list of skills that a father or father figures need to learn. I'm merely focusing on those we see displayed by the lavish father in Luke 15. If they were important enough for Jesus to reveal, then they are important enough for us to revere.

A UNIQUE ROLE

We need to pause here and ask what's so special, so unique, so important about a father or father figure exhibiting these seven skills. Can a mother not provide all seven of these skills for their child? Does a father really have something distinctive to bring to the table? If we look at the list of seven best practices, some may ask whether Mum can do some of these equally well. After all, can a mother not have **fun** with their child? Can she not **affirm** them in her words and actions? Give them quality **time**? **Hug** them? Provide a great **example**? Set reasonable and life-enhancing **rules**? Provide **secure** attachment for their child or children? Is her role not just as important? The answer is, yes of course! A mother can do all these things.

For some critics, this will be the end of the story. If mums can perform these tasks, dads aren't needed. Such critics will continue to promote the anti-fatherhood mantra of the late twentieth century and insist that a father's role is not essential. However, anyone who still claims this needs to know that they are wholly out of step with the latest peer-reviewed studies about dads. Over the last ten to fifteen years there has been a growing body of significant research into what's called 'the science of fatherhood.' Leading the way has been an influential anthropologist called Dr Anna Machin at the University of Oxford.[4] Using the latest neuroscientific data, she has proposed the same claims that in Dad School we have derived from Scripture – that a father plays a unique and vital role in the raising of children.

Before summarising her findings, I need to outline the

differences between Dr Machin's views and what we teach at Dad School. Dr Machin is an evolutionary anthropologist. She believes that the reason why dads have an essential role in parenting is the result of evolution. At Dad School, we believe that God plays a part in this process – that fatherhood is not the result of necessary developments within human biology. Our view is that human families need good fathers because this is God's plan. 'Father' is the Christian's primary name for God. When Dr Machin draws attention to the way dads' brains are hard-wired for fatherhood – something she does brilliantly – our view is that while we may differ on the reasons why this is so, we see no great divorce between faith and science in the way we talk about a father's role.

This why we hold that there is much we can learn from Dr Machin's work. She has shown that invested fathers play a unique role. She concedes that this is not something dads realise, nor is it something that society yet fully acknowledges. But the data about what happens to men after their first child is compelling proof.

Dr Machin reveals that after his first child, a father experiences significant changes in his brain. Neuroscientists have detected in new dads a measurable increase in white and grey matter in the neocortex. The neocortex is the conscious and cognitive part of the brain. It's where problems are solved, and plans are made. New mums, on the other hand, experience an increase in the limbic core of the brain, where affectionate feelings and a desire to nurture are fostered. This leads to men and women taking on different roles. While the peak activity in Mum's brain leads her to turn inwards, holding and comforting her child, the peak activity in Dad's brain leads him to turn outwards, helping his child to look at the big wide world and to interact socially with others. Dad's brain leads him to say, "You can always come back to me for a hug, but in the meantime go." It leads him to say, "I love you, and I am your secure foundation, but turn around. Look out there at the world. There's so much to discover. So much to fix."

Dr Machin says that these differences are the result of evolution.

We say God's involved too. A dad's brain is hardwired to assume this distinctive role because God – who is "our Father in heaven" – understands fatherhood better than anyone, and this is the way he has planned it. Dads are primed to parent, just like mums. But dads have been shaped to do this in a distinctive way.

GOOD DADS EVOLVE

What the science of fatherhood has revealed is that male human brains have an extraordinary plasticity. They have developed so that they can adapt to the new challenges of fatherhood. After their first child is born, their neocortices experience heightened activity. This not only means they can help their child to solve problems. It also means that they as dads can do the same. Dads too can plan, interact, fix things, and so on. They too can meet the challenges of life.

This is why Dad School is so important. Historically, courses for dads have been few and far between. Dad School is our response to this lack of learning opportunities. We stress again, although a dad's brain is primed to adapt, this does not mean a man is somehow a born or natural father. The skills of good fathering need to be learned over time. Put another way, we do not believe that fatherhood is the result of purely natural processes, but we do believe that dads evolve. Men become better dads as they learn to exercise the seven skills. They do this by utilizing the same area of their brain that has been so active in helping their child to solve problems and to interact with others. In this learning process, men acknowledge that they are works in progress and commit to becoming better dads with God's help.

At Dad School, we accordingly rely on what's come to be called the four stages of learning.[5] They look like this:

Stage 1: Unconscious Incompetence

In this early stage, you're not conscious or aware how incompetent you are as a dad. Although it sounds harsh, sometimes the pathway to true change comes when we honestly acknowledge how badly we are doing. This leads to the next phase.

Stage 2: Conscious Incompetence
In the second stage of learning, dads are made aware of the fact that they're failing. At this point they can either adopt a pessimistic and negative stance, or they can turn outwards rather than inwards and see this as a challenge to accept.

Stage 3: Conscious Competence
In the third stage of learning, dads start to become aware of what they need to do better. They become conscious of the seven skills they need to learn, and they set their minds to the task, practicing the skills with diligence and self-discipline.

Stage 4: Unconscious Competence
Someone once said that triumph is the combination of try and oomph! After a lot of trying, and a fair bit of oomph, dads become so good at the seven skills that they're not even aware how competent they have come. They triumph over adversity.

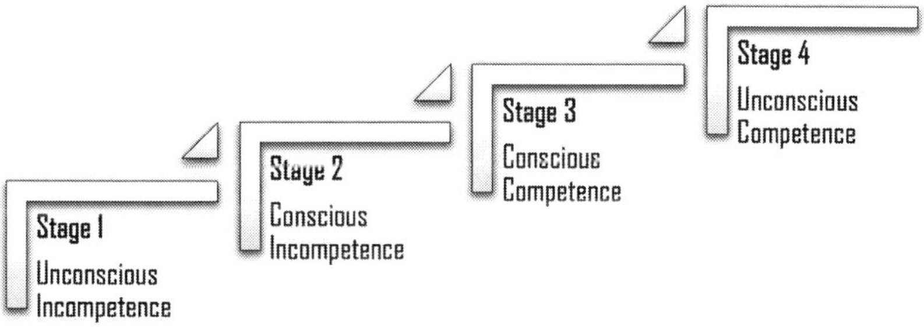

BLACK BOX THINKING

It's important at this point to acknowledge the fact that as dads we are going to fail. I'm sorry to be the bearer of bad news, but it's the truth. Being a dad is not unlike being a passenger jet. Even in this technologically advanced age, no jet is 100% perfect. People said the Titanic was the perfect ship. Some even went on to exhibit the very summit of pride and foolishness, claiming that not even God could sink it. Yet it hit an iceberg and the rest, as they say, is history. It's important therefore to be humble and realistic. There's no such thing as a perfect passenger jet. There are going to be moments when some systems fail. These minor failures can most often be rectified while the jet is in flight. The passengers don't even need to know about it. At other times, failures need more serious attention and require an unscheduled landing. On very rare occasions, there can be such a major failure that the aircraft crashes and there are casualties.

Being a dad can be a bit like this. We want to be the perfect father, but, in the end, we need to admit that only God is the perfect Father, as Jesus revealed. In fact, Jesus described human fathers not just as imperfect but downright evil at times, certainly in comparison with our Heavenly Father.[6] So, let's be humble and realistic. No dad should ever behave as if they have completely mastered and perfected the art of fatherhood. Men who present as such are not just annoying, they are deluded. The truth is, dads fail. Most often, these are small fails – ones that can be quickly rectified. At other times, a dad may need to pause, acknowledge that they have messed up, and enrol in something like Dad School to conduct a reset. On occasions, a dad may fail in a very big way, and there may be casualties. When this happens, dads will need to rise from the wreckage with a determination not only to be healed from those systemic flaws that led to the crash, but also to bring healing to those affected by their fall.

Trust me.

I know what I'm talking about here.

I have failed as a dad.

But I have also learned from my mistakes.

Matthew Syed has written a bestselling book called *Black Box*

Thinking. He points out that when passenger jets crash, the two black boxes are retrieved from the crash zone. They are studied forensically to see what went wrong. Some experts examine the box that records the inflight conversations within the cockpit. Others look at the box that records the data from the aircraft's systems. When all the reasons for the crash have been identified, the lessons are communicated throughout the airline industry, and corrections and changes that these failures reveal are made to every aircraft of the same type. That's called harnessing failure in a positive way.[7]

If you're a dad, one of the things you're going to have to learn to do is engage in a bit of black box thinking from time to time. There will be moments when you fail. Hopefully these will be so small and discrete that no one on board your family, as it were, even notices that they have occurred. But whether the mistakes are small or large, the important thing is to study what's happened, why it's happened, to learn all the lessons you need to learn, and to implement the necessary changes throughout your world. When you do, you harness failure in a positive way. Best of all, for those around you, you end up being a safer space and a more reliable, trustworthy presence.

FEELING AFRAID

All this talk of airplane disasters has most likely made some of you feel queasy or uneasy. Some people are already afraid of flying, even though we have all been told time and time again that it's by the far safest mode of travel, and that you're more likely to be attacked by a shark than experience a plane crash. I know a young father who is terrified of flying. This is partly his own fault. He watches and rewatches every episode of the long-running TV series *Air Crash Investigation*. This probably explains why he is reluctant to take his family abroad on holiday. On the rare occasions he agrees to fly with them to another, warmer country, he needs to be partially sedated to get there.

I'm not minimising this fear of flying any more than the fears men often feel about becoming a dad. I remember when I was about to become a dad for the first time. I was convinced I was going to make a mess of it. Watching the government's film about becoming a father just made it worse. I can still see the young dad at the birth. His face was white, his brow was furrowed, and his hippy hair looked as frazzled as he did. I was already fearful, but after watching a man about to have a panic attack, I came away terrified.

The only thing that helped calm me down was a film that went on general release in the cinema. It just so happened that as I was preparing to become a dad for the first time a blockbuster comedy called *Three Men and a Baby* was showing. Feeling in need of some laughs, I went to the cinema to see it. It was hilarious watching these three dudes making such a mess of trying to look after a baby. I came away feeling far more reassured than I had watching the government's film. I thought to myself, "I may make a mess of being a dad, but at least I won't make as much of a mess as those three guys!"

Being afraid of becoming a dad is common in men. In fact, it's so common, there ought to be a technical word for it. Yes, we're excited, but if we're being vulnerable, we will admit that our excitement is mixed with feelings of anxiety and even fear. Perhaps "nervous apprehension" is a better way to put it. If you identify with this, the good news is this: you're not going to be a perfect father, so stop being afraid of not living up to an expectation that nobody has of you. You'll have your flaws, and you will have moments when you're intimate with failure, but God is very forgiving when we say sorry, and so are our children. As dads, we can harness our failures in positive ways. In the process, we can pass through the four stages of learning and, with God's help, transition from incompetence to competence.

So, if your primary fear is a fear of failure, remember that it's not the falling that counts. It's rising to your feet and resolving to start again. That's what really matters.

And remember as a dad to open your heart more and more to your Heavenly Father's love. His perfect love drives out fear. When that happens, we can start to father our children from a place of love, not a place of fear. Try to avoid fathering from a centre of fear. Resolve as a dad to live from a centre of love.

THE BATTLE IS ON

Please understand as a dad that your growth from unconscious incompetence to unconscious competence is not just an isolated process. You're part of a much bigger picture. Your mission to become a better dad with God's help is a vital part of a big battle between darkness and light. For over one hundred years, there has been a consistent and brutal onslaught against fatherhood. If we just take the UK context for a moment, during World War 1, over one million British fathers lost their lives, and an equal number returned from the battlefields of Europe so traumatised that they lived in a constant state of fear. This quite naturally undermined their ability to father their children. This was followed of course by World War 2, which had equally dire consequences for dads and their children, and then by various political and ideological movements in the post-war years which succeeded in undermining the role of fathers within the home.[8]

By the time the twenty-first century began, many people were beginning to talk about fatherlessness, so much so that today it is almost a cliché in sociological and political circles. They were also commenting on the catastrophic consequences for children growing up without a dad. These covered almost all areas of life – from mental ill health to criminal behaviour. Today, the far-reaching and toxic results of fatherlessness are both well-known and well documented. There is no need to repeat them. I have written about them frequently during the last thirty years in books from *The Father You've Been Waiting For* to *I am your Father*. But I'm just one voice among many.

This brings us to Dad School. We want to state something right at the outset: *our focus is not on the terrible effects of the absence of a father. Rather, our focus is on the wonderful benefits of his presence in a child's life.*

And not just biological fathers either. We believe that the word "father" needs to be understood in a holistic sense. In other words, we argue that all kinds of invested father figures can play a part in reversing the dark tide of fatherlessness:

- Biological fathers
- Adoptive fathers
- Stepfathers
- Foster fathers
- Stand-in fathers (e.g., a coach, or a teacher)
- Spiritual fathers
- Substitute fathers (e.g., a grandfather or a godfather)

In all seven cases, people who find themselves in these paternal roles can choose to evolve in their skills, thereby helping to fulfil the promise made by the prophet Malachi in the very last words of the Old Testament. In Malachi 4:5-6, the prophet declared, "Behold, I am going to send you Elijah the prophet before the coming of the great and terrible day of the LORD. He will restore the hearts of the fathers to their children and the hearts of the children to their fathers, so that I will not come and smite the land with a curse."

How we need to see this restoration of the hearts of fathers to their children, and the hearts of children to their fathers. Dad School is one small vehicle for delivering this vision.

AN ARMY OF HEROES

Let's return to where we began – with Arnie! Back in the days when I was the senior pastor of a large church in England, one of the young people in my congregation came back from school to his parents. As they sat down to have family tea, the father asked his son, "What have you been doing today."

"A school project," the boy replied.

"What was the subject?"

"It was a question, dad." Dad waited for him to elaborate. "The teacher asked us to write a short essay answering the question, who's your hero?"

The father asked, "And who did you write about?"

"You, Dad," the boy replied.

The father beamed. Still smiling, he started to fish for compliments. "And why did you write about me?"

The boy munched some food, swallowed it, then in a matter-of-fact manner gave the answer.

"Because I couldn't spell Arnold Schwarzenegger."

How we laughed when that story went around the church!

All invested fathers are heroes in the battle for the revival of fatherhood. If they are people filled with God's love, they are part of the fulfilment of the promise we find in Malachi 4:6. They are heroes who give themselves to the great cause of restoration in the world – the restoration of the hearts of the fathers to their children, and the hearts of the children to their fathers.

Just as I was finishing this chapter, the international press reported a story about a hero father. A Russian man called Aleksei Moskalyov is the single-parent father of a daughter, now 13, called Masha. He had written comments on social media in which he spoke out against the Russian invasion of Ukraine and the war that is now costing hundreds of thousands of lives. His daughter had been drawing similarly courageous pictures at school with the slogan 'No to War.' After ten years of being raised alone by her dad, it seems she had started following his example. This has got them both into a lot of trouble. Dad, who is on the run, has been sentenced to two years in prison and his daughter has been put in an orphanage.

Masha penned a letter to her dad which her dad's lawyer has published. It has gone viral. In it, she asks her father to remain calm in the face of this adversity. She adds, "I love you so much and you should know that you did nothing wrong. I'll always be on your side, and I believe everything you do is right. When you're feeling bad or anxious, I feel sick and bad too. I believe that things are going to be fine and that we'll be together someday. I hope for the best and love you so much."

She concluded with some stirring words.

"I am proud. Yes, Dad, I can say that I am proud of my father. A dignified, smart, handsome, unyielding man who loves his daughter so much. I love you. You're a hero. My hero."

There are genuine father heroes in the world today.

They are everywhere.

And they are mostly unsung.

Take heart. As you work hard to become a better dad with God's help, you don't do this alone. You are part of a growing army of dads. Even better, you are filled with your Heavenly Father's wisdom and power. Like Arnold Schwarzenegger, you have extraordinary resources. You are filled with God's mighty power.

You are a true Turbo Man.

QUESTION TIME

Look at the four stages of learning:

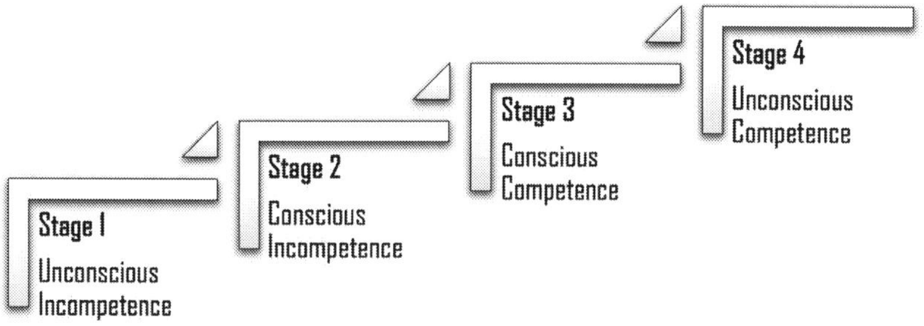

Where are you right now as an evolving father?

How are you going to get to the next stage of your development?

What practical changes are you going to make in the light of what you've just read?

F IS FOR FUN

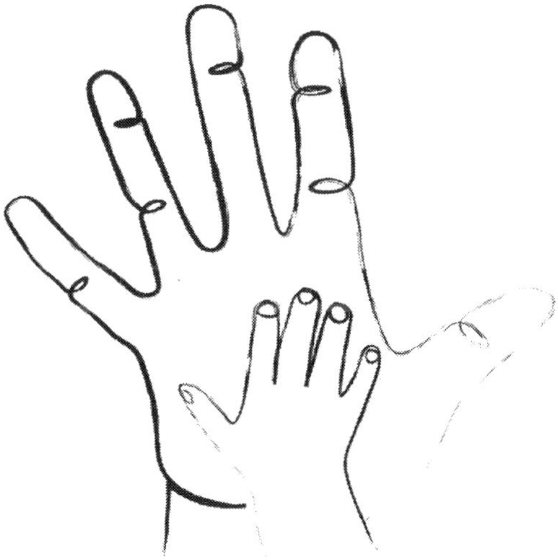

Being a father means you need to think fast on your feet. You must be judicious, wise, brave, tender, and willing to put on a frilly hat and sit down to a pretend tea party.

Matthew Buckley

2
F IS FOR FUN

One of the best games my dad ever invented was something called Kick the Can. We played it on a beach during the summer months in a place called Holkham in North Norfolk – that's on the UK's stunning east coastline. We would drive and park up before walking to the sand dunes and making base camp. Those who were feeling energetic would then march over a long stretch of flat sand to the breakers. We would swim, snorkel, and mess about in a small rubber dinghy before walking all the way back to the dunes. There Mum would be waiting with a picnic lunch. When our food had "gone down" (as my mother put it), Dad would find a suitable location nearby and invite us to play Kick the Can. My brother, twin sister, and I would need no persuasion. We would squeal with joy and then run to join in the fun.

The rules of the game were simple. Dad would find a spot of open ground surrounded by undulating dunes. He would stand in the middle of the sand and tell us to get ready. Next, he would take an empty can of soda from our picnic lunch and place it at his feet. He would tell us to go and hide while he turned his back and counted to fifty. We would run to the higher ground. Finding cover, we would shelter from the sun beneath one of the gnarly pine trees, their payload of cones and needles lying all around us on the ground. We would always take care not to stand on them. They were sharp.

After that, the fun would start.

The rules at this point were minimal. My siblings and I would watch from our separate locations in the dunes, hiding within the long green Marram grass. I remember how prickly that could be against my soft young skin. I never complained. The pleasure of the game outweighed the pain of the blades.

Sometimes I would just stay undercover for a while, sniffing the scent of the pine, enjoying the cooling effect of the breeze in the trees, letting the sand pass between my fingers. In those moments, it was as if time stood still. The only thing that would arouse me from my dreamlike state would be the sound of a seagull overhead, or our Black Labrador barking at us, giving away our location.

If we managed to remain undetected, we would wait till Dad was facing in another direction. One by one we would dash from our hiding places and try to reach the can and kick it before he saw us. If he did, the punishment always evoked a groan. It would mean having to go back to the dunes and start all over again. But if one of us succeeded, the sense of joy was indescribable. Dad would fall to the sand and pretend to be incapacitated by our victorious sprint. The victor, meanwhile, would lift the can in the air like a trophy.

CAUSING A RUMPUS

Looking back at those pastimes – or past times - I feel nothing but admiration for my adoptive father. Somehow, he had managed to create a game that required *minimum* effort from him, and *maximum* effort from us. This was nothing short of genius, especially after a picnic. It would mean he never got indigestion.

Kick the Can wasn't the only game Dad played. Another I remember is something I am confident was one of his own concoctions, or something his own father had played with him, something peculiar to our family. It was called "Rumpus" - a noun meaning a noisy disturbance or commotion. It's not a word I hear these days. It's slightly archaic, which makes it even more special. You occasionally stumble upon it in older children's stories. One memorable example is *Where the Wild Things Are* (1963). Max issues the command, "Let the wild rumpus start!" In 1930s America, spaces for messy play with children were often called rumpus rooms.

In our house, Rumpus took place after bath time and before going to bed. Dad would call us into the parental bedroom. He would be on the bed, and we would all join him. When he shouted "Rumpus," he would try and push each one of us off the bed. We would resist his attempts and climb all over him, trying to push him off. Sometimes he would remove all of us and win. Other times, he would slowly slide off the bed onto the carpet, his groans of defeat lost in our yells of triumph. Those were great moments of fun, just like Kick the Can.

Looking back fifty years later, I smile at the variety as well as the inventiveness of the way Dad had fun with us. On long car journeys, he would engage us in song. "Ten green bottles hanging on a wall" was one of his favourites, but he had a good repertoire and knew how to stave off the boredom. He was a lot of fun.

GOING FISHING

One of my fondest memories is when I was about seven years old. Dad asked if I wanted to go fishing. He often went with my older brother, but he must have now deemed me mature enough to have a go. This was both an honour and a challenge. Ours wasn't the sedentary kind of fishing where people just sit in a chair and read while they wait for a fish to bite. This was proper fishing. Fishing where you stalk your prey in the clear streams and stagnant brooks. Fishing where you need to set the right fly – dry or wet. Fishing where you need to cast with skill, the fly alighting just above the place where you've spotted a fish, then drifting on the surface downstream, directly over them.

I said yes.

Dad kitted me out with a flyfishing rod and then drove my brother and me to a river nearby.

It was early evening when we arrived, and the sun was beginning to turn a warm, golden colour in the sky. The Mayfly, recently hatched, were dropping on the surface of the river like flecks of rain. Dad pointed to the tell-tale circles forming in the water which told us where the trout were rising. To this day, I can identify where the trout are in a river because of the lessons he taught that day.

It was enormous fun.

And exciting.

Not only did we catch several rainbow trout. I also saw my first kingfisher. As we blended quietly with our surroundings, it appeared on the opposite bank. I had never seen a bird with such vibrant markings. I have not seen one like it since. It was like an epiphany.

That glorious fishing expedition, under the setting sun, lives to this day in my memory.

I am so glad I had a fun-loving dad.

WE NEED A BIGGER BOAT!

Even in a crisis, dad was fun. Like the time when a fishing trip was cut short. He and I were in a rowing boat on a huge salt-water loch off the north-east coast of Scotland. We had decided to go out one evening to catch some mackerel. We stopped at a point where there was no current and put out our lines. About ten minutes later, having caught several mackerel and thrown back a scorpion fish, I heard something in the water nearby. I put down my rod and turned in the direction of the noise. There, gliding through the water, was an enormous dorsal fin. It was dark and forbidding, and yet I wasn't scared. That's the thing about being with your dad. You always believe you're safe, even when a shark is cruising near your boat.

I pointed to the fin.

"What's that, Dad?"

I am sure, looking back across the entire sweep of my childhood, that this was the only time I ever saw any hint of alarm on my father's otherwise calm façade. He took one look at the dorsal fin, and the caudal fin that was now trailing behind it above the surface. He could see that the fish was twice the size of our clinker-built boat. He had no idea what kind of creature it was. He was not a marine biologist so he couldn't have known that it was a harmless basking shark, a fish that ate plankton not people. But he made his decision.

"I think we'd better go back, my son."

Gripping the oars, he rowed as calmly as he could while I sat at the stern of the boat leaning over the gunwales staring at the great fin as it drifted off towards the farthest shore.

When we returned to the holiday house, Dad explained why we were back early. We all laughed. I'm still laughing now as I write. Dad could appreciate the comedy in a crisis.

THE FIRST SKILL

I'm so pleased that the acrostic for Dad School – F.A.T.H.E.R.S – starts with the word FUN. If there's one thing all fathers should learn it's this: they have a unique role when it comes to fun, play, and games. When dads invest in exercising the skill of fun, they have no idea what memories they are creating, what legacies they are leaving, or what benefits they are producing in their child's life. Some of the most lasting and lifegiving lessons are communicated not through sermonizing but in contexts where dads have a laugh with their children. These sessions of histrionics and hysterics can often teach a child far more than those moments when a dad indulges in moralizing.

This brings me back to the ideal father in Luke 15. You remember the story. The younger son demands his inheritance. The father is amazingly patient and kind. He says yes. The boy goes off to a remote, heathen territory and wastes it all on hedonistic living. When he comes to his senses, he returns home, only to find that his dad has been waiting for him all these years. There is a poignant and beautiful reunion, followed by the father's command to his servants.

"Bring the fattened calf and kill it. Let's have a feast and celebrate. For this son of mine was dead and is alive again; he was lost and is found.' So, they began to celebrate.

As you read these words, make a note of the word "celebrate." It's used twice in a short space of time. In the original language, it means literally to "make merry."

This dad organises a huge party – one large enough for the entire village, which probably numbered around 200 people. He instructs the servant to build an enormous barbeque. The whole community is to enjoy prime roast beef.

And be merry!

Why does he do this? Because he's over the moon. He is happy beyond words that his boy has returned. He thought his boy was lost, dead even. But now he's found. He's alive! So, the dad is lavish, excessive, generous in the party he throws. He's the prodigal one, if you take the word "prodigal" literally. There is music and dancing. There's a feast to be shared. Dad has spent a fortune. But money isn't the issue for him, which is why he doesn't ask the boy to pay him back through a lifetime of service. He spares no expense to hold what was probably the finest celebration the villagers had ever seen.

What a fun-loving, party-throwing dad.

And the good news is this.

The dad in the story represents what God is really like. He's a fun-loving, party-throwing Dad too. Whenever one of his lost boys or girls comes home into his arms of love, he rejoices over them with singing. He spins around and dances with joy. He tells heaven to hold the party of all parties. He is therefore not the stern, remote, humourless judge that religious people have made him out to be. He is the joy bringer. He is the one who anoints our heads with the oil of gladness. Why? Because he knows that the joy of the Lord is our strength!

If you've not had an earthly father who has had fun with you, if you've never had a dad who played something like Kick the Can with you, understand this: you have a Father in heaven who's crazy about you, who loves spending time with you, who longs to make merry with you. Don't be like the older son who reacted against such an idea. Don't be like the teachers of the Law – the ones listening to Jesus's story – who wanted a legalistic, angry God. Learn to connect with your merry-making Maker, your celebratory Creator, your fun-loving Father. He'll make up the fun deficit if you didn't get that from your own dad. He'll change your garment of despair for a mantle of praise.

CHEMICAL REACTIONS

In the last chapter, I introduced you to the vital research of Dr Anna Machin of the University of Oxford. She has shown from scientific data that fathers have a distinctive part to play in the raising of children. Fathers and mothers bring something different to the table. The evidence provided by neuroscientific research – especially research into activity in the human brain – confirms this. When a couple has a baby, the dad's brain reacts differently. While the mother experiences peak activity in the limbic core (the part where feelings of affection and nurturing are enhanced) a father experiences peak activity in the neocortex (the part where cognition and planning are generated). A mum wants to hold and soothe her child. A dad wants to help his child to navigate the challenges of the outside world.

When it comes to fun, we see even more fascinating differences between dads and mums. No one is saying that mothers can't and don't have meaningful fun with their children. A mother's play is important too. But when it comes to dads, the skill of having fun with their children seems to have an extraordinarily beneficial effect on both. When a father plays with his child even for a short time, there is a massive release of chemicals in both his and his child's brain. They both experience a rush of chemicals like dopamine (which create a feel-good sensation) and oxytocin (which enhances bonding), to name just two. This means that even a short dose of Kick the Can, Rumpus, or fishing can create enormous benefits. God, who is the Perfect Father, has hard-wired a dad's brain in such a way that he gets a big benefit from a little play. That's time efficiency for you!

And it's borne out by my own story. One of my most precious memories is of an incident when I was four. Dad was in the garden. I held his hand and asked him to run with me.

He agreed.

The next few seconds were euphoric.

While holding onto my hand, he began to accelerate. Within seconds, I was going so fast my feet were off the ground. Before I knew it, I was horizontal, still connected, but flowing in his slipstream, travelling faster than I had ever been. Flying almost.

Not even my first take off in a passenger jet (which happened three years later) was as exhilarating.

Not even the fastest, most stomach-churning rides at Disney World were as breath-taking.

It was the rush of a lifetime.

I'm sure Dad felt it too.

THE BENEFITS OF PLAY

At this point, some of you may be saying, "This is a bit unfair. Dads get all the fun. They even get a rush of amazing chemicals in their brains. And that's just from minimum effort!" If you're thinking that, don't fret! Mums also get a similar rush of chemicals, it's just that don't get it from play and fun. They get a release of dopamine and oxytocin when they hold and cuddle their child. This is why a child will run to Mum when they're crying and need soothing, but they will rush to Dad when they want to be held aloft and treated like an airplane! Dr Machin says this is the way we have evolved. At Dad School, we see this as part of God's plan, and these don't need to be either-or.

All this is very revealing, but at the same time I don't want you to think that the only reason why dads should have fun with their children is because it will give both parties involved a pleasant flood of chemicals. As a result of a great deal of research we now know the benefits of this kind of father-child activity are more far-reaching than a biochemical high. Consider the following:

A) Behavioural Benefits

When a dad plays with his child, it establishes boundaries for aggression. In fact, rough-and-tumble play is the best way a dad can teach their child what the limits are when it comes to aggressive behaviour. When a child goes too far – say, through biting or hitting – a father can press the pause button and explain that what the child has done has hurt him and that he'll have to stop playing if it happens again. This sets boundaries. Fun with dad is therefore a great – possibly the best - way for establishing controls on aggression.

B) Social Benefits

When a dad plays with his children, he is teaching vital lessons about social interaction. These can be anything from reading another person's intentions to understanding how everyone is different and that these differences need to be respected in reciprocal behaviour. When dads play with their kids, the fun communicates vital life lessons that help immeasurably in the development of a child's social skills. It also helps with a child's language. When dads play sensitively with their children in the first three years, it enhances linguistic skills.

C) Emotional Benefits

Dad play teaches a child about emotional intelligence. As a professor of play in education has said (this time from the University of Cambridge): "Physical play creates fun, exciting situations in which children need to apply self-regulation... It's a safe environment in which children can practise how to respond. If they react the wrong way, they might get told off, but it's not the end of the world – and next time they might remember to behave differently."[9] When a dad spends quality play time with their child, there are long-term emotional benefits.

Fathers therefore have a unique role when it comes to having fun. It truly is a skill worth developing.

A COMMITMENT TO LEARN

I'd like to repeat what I said in the last chapter about the myth of the "born father" or the "gifted dad." At Dad School, we don't believe that a person is a "natural" father, nor that there's some supernatural endowment of fatherhood. People become dads over time as they practice the skills in this book. In the learning journey, we start out unconsciously incompetent – unaware of how incapable we are as a dad, ignorant of how poorly we are doing. But, over time, we make progress towards becoming unconsciously competent – unaware of how capable and skilful we have become. The key is to be determined to do the right thing, and to do the thing right. If you have a firm commitment to becoming a better dad with God's help, then I'm confident you will achieve this vital and lifechanging goal.

This is as true for the skill of fun as it is for all the other six skills of fathering that we will look at in this book. Everyone starts on the same level playing field when it comes to having fun with their kids. We are not born with some special ability to have fun, nor do we have access to some special mystical gift of play. The only advantage we may have is a generational blessing – the blessing of having a dad who was good at having fun with us, no doubt because his own dad was good at having fun with him. If that's our backstory, we will have the example of a positive role model we can emulate.

In my own case, I was very blessed to have an adoptive dad who excelled in this skill of having fun. When I came to be a young father of four children (not all at once, but one at a time!), I decided to base my play on what my dad had done. I engaged in a version of Kick the Can with my kids in the same sand dunes in which I had played. I came up with a remix of Rumpus too. Seeing how well these went gave me confidence to try my own inventions.

So, to take one example, I upgraded Rumpus into a survival game. The bed was a raft. The floor was shark-infested waters. I was a nasty selfish person trying to push my kids off the raft. I'm not sure that the message was all that healthy. I would never have done such a thing in real life. But my kids loved it. After bath time, Rumpus would meet Jaws. We would laugh ourselves silly.

After that was done, my children would often ask me for a story. "Tell us about Michael the Teddy Bear!" Michael the Teddy Bear was a character I'd invented – a bear with a somewhat nervous temperament who would often find himself in challenging circumstances. Whenever he was in danger, he would become apprehensive and break wind. My children loved the sound effects!

There's a lesson here. Besides the obvious one that kids love blowing raspberries, there's the importance of playing to your strengths. My strength is telling stories. Your strength may be in music, or maths, or making things. Whatever skills you have, use these. You may not have had a fun-loving dad, but you do have things in your life that are fun. Make these the resources for your play.

MAKING UP THE DEFICITS

If you never had a father who showed you how to have fun, I have two suggestions that I hope will help.

The first is to lean on God. As you build your connection with the perfect Father in heaven, draw upon his resources too. Remember the story in Luke 15 – the sacred text on which all our fathering principles are ultimately derived in this book. That extraordinary character was a fun-loving, party-throwing dad. That father in turn is a picture of what God the Father is really like. He is not a remote and miserable deity. He is a relational and merrymaking daddy! Your connection with this fun-loving Father will help you in your play times.

Dad School is about becoming a better dad *with God's help*, so ask your Heavenly Father to help you. Pray something like this: "Dear Father, please help me to be better at having fun with my child. Help me to play with them in a way that enhances their development. Make me a dad after your own heart. I ask this in Jesus's name."

That's the first key.

The second is to ask for help from other dads who have moved towards the unconsciously competent end of the spectrum. If you've not had a father or father figure in your life who's acted as a positive role model in this skill, find ones who do.

One of the summer Bible camps I used to attend as a regular speaker provided a wonderful example of this. My good friend Dave, who ran the camps with his wife Mandy, used to have tent meetings in the morning and the evening, but not in the afternoons. This was because he wanted to encourage people to have family times. Dave was particularly intentional about asking dads to invest time in playing with their kids during the spaces in the camp schedule.

On one occasion, a young dad came up to Dave. "I'm no good at playing with my kids. I've just never had any role model for this. Can you help me?" At that very moment, another dad was walking past them. Dave knew that this guy was good at playing with his kids. Dave asked if he would take the other dad under his wing and show him. The guy said yes. The dad who felt consciously incompetent spent the afternoon with him. After seeing how to do it, he started to move from conscious incompetence towards conscious competence.

If you have a deficit of role models for this skill, pray for your Heavenly Father to equip you. And ask another dad to show you. Remember, when it comes to fatherhood, God doesn't call the equipped. He equips the called!

PLAYING REMOTELY

I want to give a shoutout to those who are trying to be better dads while they're away from their children. This may be for many reasons, but one can be especially painful and challenging. This is when dads are in prison. One of the things that can cause incarcerated fathers immense mental torment is being separated from their children and therefore unable to be present to them day and night. Shaming and blaming such fathers is completely unhelpful here, so please refrain from condemning people who are going through this. I have shared the message of the Father's love in packed men's prisons in the USA and the UK and I can tell you that approximately 85% of these incarcerated men – especially young men – have never had a loving father in their lives to give them not only a good example but also vital lessons how to stay out of trouble. This father hunger is one of their main motivations for wanting to be a good dad to their own children. They simply don't want to perpetuate generational patterns of absenteeism.

I think it is instructive and important here to say that Dad School started out as a course designed for UK prisons. I was commissioned to create a learning module to help incarcerated men to engage in long-distance fathering. Given that so much crime committed in the UK is attributable at least in part to fatherlessness in the lives of the perpetrators, this seemed to me a no-brainer. However, several factors both before and during the pandemic put a spanner in the works. Although I had written an early version of Dad School – one designed for prisons – and although there was a team in place ready to implement it, various obstacles meant that this vital initiative had to be put on hold. One of the dreams those of us who are running Dad School harbour is this, that one day we will be able to return to the original vision and take this course into prisons.

When I was writing the prison-friendly version of Dad School a few years ago, I thought long and hard about how dads in prison could ever exercise the skill of fun with their kids. The only opportunities they had were on the days their families were allowed to visit them. But the rest of the time, it seemed to me to be impossible for them to be at play with their daughters and sons.

Until, that is, I discovered a charity called Storybook Dads. In a nutshell, this is an organization dedicated to recording imprisoned dads telling stories (video, not just audio), which their children can watch and listen to at bedtime. This allows children to hear their daddy's voice every night before they fall asleep, even though he is unable to be with them in person. After the dads have recorded their stories, teams of people edit out the mistakes and add music before sending these out to the children. The genius of the project is this: these editorial teams are prisoners trained by Storybook Dads![10]

This bold and brilliant initiative is not only relieving the angst felt by fathers. It is also reducing the separation anxiety felt by children. All in all, Storybook Dads is a great example of out-of-the-box thinking. It shows how with a little ingenuity people can engage in long-distance fathering where the skill of fun and the practice of play can be done excellently and effectively. As one mum wrote when she was sharing with the team responsible for Storybook Dad:

"Now when they ask for daddy I can put on a disc, and they can see and hear him - which they were unable to do before and used to have loads of tears and tantrums.

They especially loved the Christmas one where their daddy was dressed up as Santa. We watched it together on Christmas Day. It helped them feel close to him on such a special day.

I can't thank you enough for that."

STAND-IN FATHERS

I also want to champion all those men who step into the gap left by an absent father. There are so many children growing up without a father. I'm thinking right now of a boy aged ten whose dad has been absent most of his life. That absentee is his biological father and nothing more. He's one of those men who make women pregnant, but then abdicate their responsibilities when the child is born. These men just confirm the time-honoured mantra that it is all too easy to become a father, but it's much harder to be a dad. Pretty well any old fool can inseminate a woman, and regularly does, but it takes a wise man to provide a healthy male role model for their children.

I meet this very gifted ten-year-old boy quite a lot now and whenever I do, the one thing he always wants to do is have fun with me. Sometimes this means powering up the Play Station. At other times, it means visiting a farm and feeding Al Pacas. Last weekend, I was launching my new novel at our local bookshop. The lad came and listened to every word I said. As people were leaving at the end, he found an old boardgame in the shop - Cluedo.

I never had a chance to say goodbye to the fans who had attended my book launch. My young friend wanted to play Cluedo with me. So that's what we did. As the guests filtered out, we started working our way around the board, pretending to be detectives working out who'd committed the murder.

We had a laugh.

And it was a kind of a rush.

Isn't this going too far? No! From her neuroscientific research, Dr Anna Machin has discovered that when a stand-in father plays with a child, he gets the same chemical feel-good and bonding reaction in his brain as a biological father does.

And the child gets it too!

It seems once again that God our Heavenly Father has not only thought of everything (he is omniscient, after all), but he's also made a man's brain so neuroplastic that it can adapt to a fatherlike role and experience the same beta-endorphin rush biological fathers experience (he is omnipotent, after all).

If there's an incentive for a healthy, stand-in dad or father figure to invest in playing, maybe this is it. God has purposed for men to receive a special reward whenever they play.

TO BOLDLY GO!

I grew up with the original Star Trek series on TV – the one that begins with the guy doing the voiceover during the dramatic music and the opening credits, the one who talks about the USS Enterprise boldly going where no man has gone before. When it comes to us fathers and father figures, it's perhaps worth saying before finishing this chapter that we may have to learn not only to meditate on these words. We may also have to activate them too.

What do I mean?

I mean that if we are to exercise the skill of fun and play, we may have to boldly go where men have historically not dared to venture - into groups dominated almost exclusively by women.

Groups like what used to be called *Mums and Toddlers*, but which are more often these days called *Parents and Toddlers*.

When I first became a father, it was in the late 1980s, and in those days church (and indeed non-church) toddler groups were women-only spaces. This was not so much a matter of official regulation as it was a consequence of tradition. This was the tail-end of an era when dads were still expected to go out to work while mums would stay at home to look after and raise their children.

As a new dad, I remember heading off to one of these groups. I was the only man there. While the mums were very sensitive and tried to make me feel at home, I still felt extremely vulnerable in that setting. The only thing to which I can compare it was the time almost three decades later when I put on weight. Being a dad can do that to you, so be warned! I decided that I would head off to my local Slimming World group. There were thirty people there. I was the only man. It was challenging enough admitting I was carrying too much freight, but trying to remedy that problem in a group where I was the lone male was very tough. That said, I stuck with it, and even on one occasion won the award for Slimmer of the Week. I lost an astonishing 1½ lbs!

Fathers and father figures may have to be prepared to boldly go where it feels like no man has ever gone before. These days, of course, it's a lot easier than it was when I was a young dad because there is much more emphasis on inclusivity. But it's still hard, which is why I really appreciate the research into fatherhood and play that's recently been conducted by the Lego Foundation. The author of a report sponsored by Lego has written that play – or what I call the skill of having fun - is one of the most vital ingredients that a dad brings to the parenting table. She also stated in her report that it's therefore extremely important for fathers and father figures to go to groups where they can interact playfully with their young child. This, however, is still a challenge. As she wrote, "Even today, it's not unusual for fathers who take their child to a parent-toddler group, for example, to find that they are the only father there. A culture shift is beginning to happen, but it needs to happen more."[11] That's my perception too.

Fathers and father figures need to release their inner Captain Kirk and boldly go. We need to explore strange new worlds, including the world of parent and toddler groups.

JUST BE YOURSELF!

As dads, we watch Jim Carrey in the film *Liar, Liar* and see him playing with his son, manipulating his hand and arm to form a claw. We hear him shout, "The claw! The claw!" and adding, "Run for your life!" We see his boy holler with delight as he flees. We think to ourselves, "I wish I could play with my kid like that."

At Christmas time, we watch *The Holiday* and see Jude Law, a widower, playing with his son and his daughter at the kitchen table. He puts a white table napkin over his head, wedging it in place with his glasses. We hear the laughter of his children – and Cameron Diaz, his admirer – and we think to ourselves, "If I can't do the Claw, let me at least do Mister Napkin Head."

We forget two things. Firstly, that these examples are from films, and films are the modern equivalent of myths and fairy tales. They are make-believe. Secondly, we fail to note that these men are not playing themselves but characters in a story. And in that one single observation there is a lifegiving lesson for fathers.

Just be yourself.

If doing "the claw" isn't you, don't do it. It'll come across as fake and silly, which is what happens when the boy's stepfather tries to do it in *Liar, Liar*. It's just embarrassing. He didn't invent the game. It's not his way of playing. He knows it. The boy knows it. And the same is true with *The Holiday*. Don't try Mister Napkin Head. As dads this is not who we are. We need to be true to ourselves. I need to be me, not a Jim Carrey or a Jude Law wannabee. You need to be you.

My adoptive dad was true to who he was.

He loved playing Kick the Can in the dunes.

He adored playing Rumpus on the bed.

He developed his own skills when it came to fun.

When I started writing this chapter, I engaged in an online discussion with my twin sister in America. I asked her if she remembered Dad playing Kick the Can with us. She said yes and followed up with her own description of her memories. I added mine.

When the conversation drew to a natural close, it did so with a remark she made.

"I'd love to do it again with him at Holkham Beach."

If I have one thing to say in conclusion, it's this. Make the most of every opportunity to play with your children. Enjoy having fun with them. Cultivate the skill of playing games and having a good laugh with them. Of all the things children remember about their dads when they grow up and grow old, it's those times you lifted them in the air and pretended they were an airplane, running around the room, dive bombing you, looping the loop with you, before ever so gently lowering you to the ground and bringing you into land.

This is what old men and women yearn for again. And in this regard, they may not fully know that they are not so much pining for their past as preparing for their future.

For what is heaven if it is not a place of joy, of play, and endless laughter – a place beyond all space and time where God our perfect Father lifts us in his arms, wipes away our tears, and fills our hearts with ecstasy in his everlasting house?

And what fun that will be!

QUESTION TIME

Look at the four stages of learning:

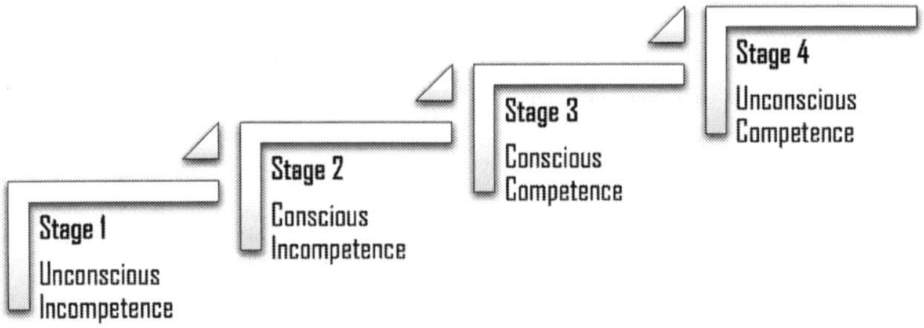

Where are you right now in the skill of having fun and playing with your children?

How are you going to get to the next stage of competence?

What practical changes are you going to make as a dad in the light of what you've just read?

A IS FOR AFFIRMATION

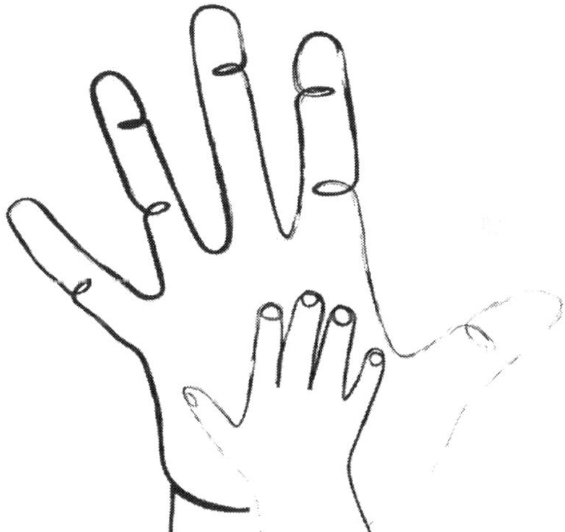

It was my father who taught me to value myself.
He told me that I was uncommonly beautiful and that
I was the most precious thing in his life.

Dawn French

3
A IS FOR AFFIRMATION

Marvyn Harrison is a British father with considerable influence among black dads in the UK, USA, and Africa.[12] It all started in 2017 when he watched other dads having affectionate moments with their kids. At that time, he had a new baby and an eighteen-month-old toddler. By his own admission, he was an absentee. Having had no father, he had no older male role model in his own backstory to inspire him. "I was basing my feelings about being a dad on the experience I had – or the lack of experience I had – with my father."

Two things challenged him. Firstly, he saw other dads embracing their kids and thought, "I don't have many of those moments." Secondly, something significant occurred in the runup to Father's Day 2018 – something that happened when he was trying to look after his baby daughter Ocean, and his son Blake.

"Ocean started crying, so I picked her up and tried to placate her. That made her cry even more. It was as if she was saying:

'Get your hands off me, where's my mother?' And then her crying alerted Blake and he was like, 'Yeah, I want my mum, too.' I had to give my daughter to her mum. My son then ran past me and jumped on to her, saying, 'Yeah! We want Mummy'."

For Marvyn, this was a defining moment. He said, "That really affected me. It didn't feel good."

One week later, it was Father's Day and Marvyn didn't feel like celebrating. He decided to send a WhatsApp message to the other black fathers he knew. There were 23 of them in the group. He wished them Happy Father's Day and added this: "I just want to thank everyone here, because I look to you when I'm thinking about how I parent and I'm finding it really difficult."

The response took him by surprise.

One by one these dads confessed that they were all looking at each other and feeling a failure. None of them knew they were doing this. They then started chatting with each other about black fatherhood. A breakthrough came when Marvyn started practicing affirmations with his son Blake. "I would make him laugh by saying: 'I am brave'." One of the reasons Marvyn did this was because he had experienced extreme racism as a child in Hackney (north London) where he was called the N-word. He said, "Telling my children that they're beautiful, they're powerful, they're loving, they're kind, is really important, because I don't think society will ever say that to them."

Today, Marvyn is the main influencer in a global movement for black fathers. His experience of practicing the skill of affirmation has led him to write a children's picture book listing the affirmations he uses with his kids. The book is called *I Love Me.*

A TRIPLE-A BLESSING

At Dad School, we passionately believe in the power of affirmation. The skill of affirmation is something fathers are called to exercise with their children. The learning process for perfecting this skill takes time. Marvyn wasn't even aware that he was incompetent. It was talking with other dads on WhatsApp that helped him to become conscious of his incompetence as a father. Instead of feeling a failure and withdrawing from his role, he started practicing the skill of affirmation. Perhaps at this point you remember what people used to say about practice. My dad said it all the time when I was a boy. "Practice makes perfect." Today, Marvyn is not only unconsciously competent in this skill. He is also training other dads to be the same.

What is affirmation? Affirmation is the expression of what I call the three A's – acceptance, approval, and affection. Affirmation is like a triple-A battery. It powers up the father-child relationship. It strengthens the child's self-esteem.

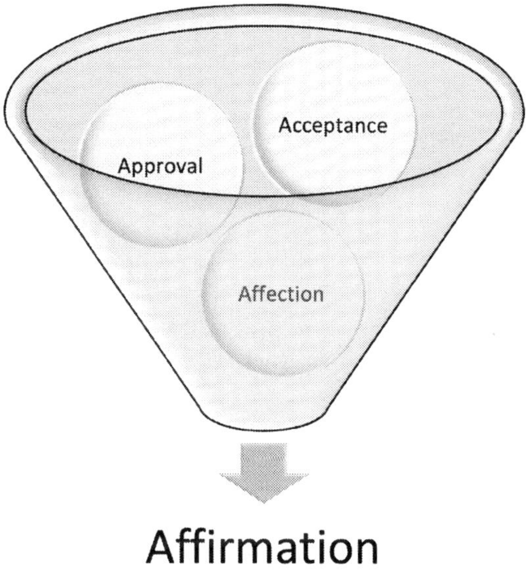

Let's look at these three A's.

Acceptance is a part of affirmation. When a father affirms their child, they are effectively saying, "I accept you. I accept you for who you are. You are my child. My love for you is unconditional."

Approval is also part of affirmation. When a father affirms their child, they are effectively saying, "I approve of you. I approve of you because you are my child. My love for you is unwavering."

Affection is also part of affirmation. When a father affirms their child, they are effectively saying, "I not only love you. I like you. I am especially fond of you. Nothing will ever change that."

A father needs to be transmitting these three A's. That said, it should not be so overused that it becomes tiresome in a child's mind. If you take your child to Disney World too often, the chances are it will lose its appeal. The same is true of affirmation. Don't overdo it, and don't force it. When the skill of affirmation is exercised in the right way (sincerely, appropriately) at the right time (when a dad can see his child needs it), it fortifies the scaffolding of self-esteem in that child's life. It shows the child that they are accepted, approved of, and given affection for who they are, not for what they do.

And that's the point.

Affirmation is not related to *performance*.

Affirmation is not something you give when a child has done well at music, sports, academics, and so on. That's not affirmation. That's applause. Applause is a response to what the child does.

Affirmation is related to *position*.

Affirmation is something you give to your child simply because they are your son or daughter. You're crazy about them for who they are. While applause is related to *doing*, affirmation is related to *being*. You revel in your child simply for who they are.

BEING AND DOING

It's important at this point to remind dads that affirmation is something that should primarily be verbalised. Dads have a unique role in telling their child that they are special, precious, cherished, and loved. All the science tells us that fathers build self-worth and significance in their child and that they do this in a unique way. This has been known for thousands of years. The ancient Jewish sage called Ben Sira put it best. He said that "a person's honour comes from their father."[13] It is dads who confer the gift and blessing of honour in a family. When dads are both present and affirming, their words of honour can reverberate in a child's soul for the rest of their lives. If a child ventures into adulthood with a strong sense that they are honoured, they are much more likely to interact kindly and positively with others, and they are much more likely to walk in a sense of destiny and purpose.

If you still need persuading, look at Jesus. When he was just over thirty years old, he knew it was time to begin his public ministry, so he went to the river Jordan to be baptised by his cousin John. When Jesus came out of the water, the Gospel records tell us that the heavens opened above his head. God the Father spoke amazing words of affirmation over his Son, telling him, "You are my Son, chosen and marked by my love, pride of my life" (Mark 1:11, *The Message*).

That's a very subversive thing to say. Many of us have had dads who only said they were proud of us when we had done something worthy of praise. But Jesus hasn't started his public ministry yet. He hasn't preached a sermon. He hasn't healed the sick. He hasn't cleansed any lepers. He hasn't raised the dead. He has *done* nothing that you'd think would merit the words, "You're the pride of my life." He's simply been God's Son, living a quiet and humble life, preparing for his launch into the public domain.

But isn't that the point?

Affirmation is in response to who you are.

Applause is in response to what you've done.

Jesus stands in the river and receives a triple-A blessing. His Father tells him that he's accepted for who he is. His Father tells him that he's approved of because of his position. And he is lavished with the affection of God because he's God's Son.

From this moment on, Jesus will work *from* approval, not *for* approval. He will have a strong sense of who he is, boldly saying to others the two key words "I am" ("I am the Bread of Life", "I am the Good Shepherd," etc). His sense of security, self-worth, and significance will never be in doubt. His identity as the Father's precious Son will be robust and indeed unshakeable. He will not wonder whether he is worthy of love and belonging.

This is the power of affirmation.

It's about being, not doing.

Dads have a unique part to play in this.

They have a vital role in exercising this skill.

Truly a person's honour comes from their father.

SHOWING AND TELLING

Affirmation is primarily a verbal gift. It's something you say to your child, as Marvyn Harrison has shown us. But it is also something that can be communicated through actions. Put simply, affirmation is something you can *show* your child not just *tell* them, and you can do this through gestures and gifts.

Everything we're teaching at Dad School ultimately has its roots in what we see the dad do in Jesus's parable in Luke 15. When his rebellious son eventually comes home, the dad in the story does two quite remarkable things.

The first is he tells his servants to go back to his house, fetch the robe, return to the boy, and drape it over his shoulders. This was an extraordinary gesture. The robe in question was something reserved for visiting dignitaries. When someone of special importance came to the village, this dad would show the guest how honoured they were by asking his servants to fetch the robe. This was not a verbal way of affirming the visitor. It was a physical gesture – an enacted message. It was not a matter of telling but a matter of showing.

Understood within its village context, this dramatic moment in the story is quite outlandish. The dad conveys his affirmation for his returning son by an act, not a word. Once that robe is covering the boy, everyone watching knows the message. It is code for, "This boy is a V.I.P. He's special. Honoured. Welcome."

The second thing he does is tell his servants to fetch the ring – also an extraordinary act. This was a signet ring owned by the father, one he intended all along to give his son. It was to be worn on the fourth finger of the boy's right hand. Once it was there, everyone in the village knew what it meant. "This boy is my son."

Perhaps you can see how affirmation is not just a verbal skill, it's a physical one as well. It's not just something a dad *tells* his child, it's something he *shows* them too.

Is there something special you possess as a dad that one day you might give to your child to show they are infinitely precious in your sight? Maybe a family heirloom, a meaningful gift?

I remember how I felt before my eighteenth birthday when my dad asked me if I wanted a family signet ring as a gift. My older brother – their biological son – had one. As an adopted child, I felt so honoured to be given one too. When Dad asked me what crest I wanted, I asked for the Cross. I am twice adopted, after all.

In exercising the skill of affirmation, don't forget to be creative. There are at least two ways you can do this. Find out what works best for your child/ren. Everyone's different. There's no one-size-fits-all approach to exercising this skill. For example, when it came to verbal affirmation, my adoptive father was much better at writing it than saying it. When I was sent away to boarding school, he would write letters to me, and at the end of one he wrote, "I am so glad I adopted you. It was the best decision I ever made."

So, be open to all forms of communication.

There are many ways to exercise this skill.

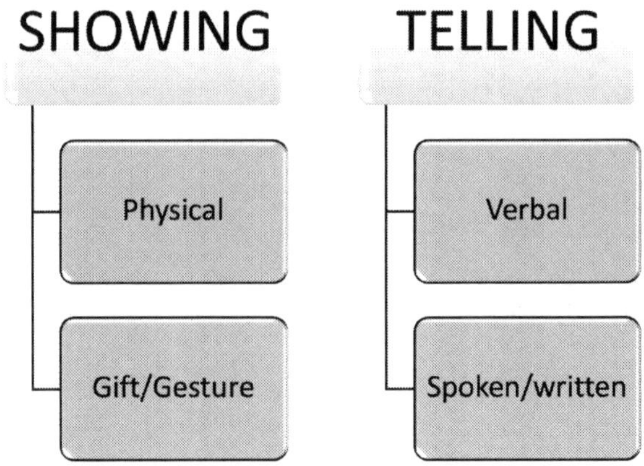

THE ANTIDOTE TO SHAME

Reading all this, you may still need some incentivizing when it comes to exercising the skill of affirmation as a dad. Maybe you were brought up in quite a stoical atmosphere where the prevailing message – spoken or unspoken – was that you should never expect to be thanked, let alone praised. Your task was simply to get on with life, do your job, and not expect any reward. If that was the kind of ethos you experienced, it can be hard to engage in this skill. You may say, "All this affirmation stuff is far too emotional."

So then, let me give you another reason for becoming unconsciously competent in the skill of affirmation. Let me ask you this: "if a person's honour comes from their father, what happens when a father is either physically or emotionally absent?" I'll tell you. The child grows up experiencing the opposite of honour. What's the opposite of honour? The answer is shame.

Most people in the West have little understanding of the twin ideas of honour and shame, so let's pause and take stock. Many Westerners confuse or conflate shame with guilt. But shame is very different from guilt, as I've written frequently in many of my books. People feel guilty about what they've done, but people feel ashamed about who they are. Guilt is what I feel when I've made a mistake. Shame is what I feel when I come to believe the lie that I *am* a mistake.[14]

Why would any child believe such a thing? The answer is because of a negative experience of being fathered.

There are many negative fathering styles today, and I've written about these in *I am your Father*. Two require special mention here – *absent* and *abusive* fathering.

Let's look at absent fathers first.

When a dad is absent from the home (through death, divorce, desertion etc), their child is deprived of honour. Lacking that constant affirmation from dad, the child grows up feeling ashamed. Shame, as Brené Brown has said, is the feeling of being unworthy of love and belonging.[15] If a child has an absent father, they not only lose a sense of honour; they also gain a sense of shame. They come to believe the toxic lie that if only they had been a better child, their dad would have been present. This is shame. They feel to blame. It is because they are somehow unlovable, ugly, defective, naughty that dad isn't around. That, of course, is a lie. We might put it this way:

The absence of a father leads to the presence of shame.

But there's another, equally traumatic scenario. When a father abuses their child – verbally, physically, emotionally, sexually, even religiously or spiritually – that child is also deprived of honour. The person who is called to be the primary honour-giver in the home has abdicated their responsibility and made the damaging decision to operate in the opposite spirit – the spirit of shame. When fathers abuse rather than affirm their children, any foundation of positive self-worth the child may have had is rocked by fissures as big as anything in an earthquake disaster movie. These acts of shaming are catastrophic; they produce cracks in the child's soul, and these can lead to increasing problems over the course of a lifetime. What we saw about an absent father is therefore also true of an abusive father.

The abuse of a father leads to the presence of shame.

This is why it's so important for dads to do be intentional about doing two things. The first is to avoid any semblance, any hint, of shaming their child. Be aware that shaming is a spectrum, with low-level harm at one end, high-level injury at the other. Many dads aren't even aware they're hurting their child. We need to consciously avoid every possibility of it. For example, never say the following.

"I'm ashamed of you."

You may be ashamed of what a child has done, but you should never be ashamed of who they are.

"Shame on you!"

Don't put shame on a child's life. Bless them with honour. Let them wear a crown of acceptance.

"You should be ashamed of yourself!"

No, they shouldn't! They should never feel shame about who they are. They are fearfully and wonderfully made!

The second thing dads should do is be intentional about conferring honour upon their child. In other words, be present, not absent. Be affirming, not abusive. As you look at the table below, make sure you are reinforcing the positive beliefs associated with honour, not the negative beliefs associated with shame.

SHAME	HONOUR
I am unworthy	I am worthy
I am unlovable	I am lovable
I am hopeless	I am hopeful
I am ordinary	I am special
I am incapable	I am capable

LARRY'S CHRISTMAS PRESENT

One of my favourite authors, Brennan Manning, once told a story about a guy called Larry.[16] Larry was not blessed with attributes most people would regard as attractive. He was overweight, covered in acne, had a bad lisp, and terrible hair. His dress sense didn't help. He didn't wear shoes and had a T-shirt that seemingly hadn't ever been washed. Worse still, Larry knew it. Whenever he looked at his reflection in the mirror, he spat at it. He felt thoroughly ashamed.

One Christmas, Larry received a present he would never forget. He was home on vacation and staying with his parents in Rhode Island. That first night he came to the family meal table smelling like a goat. His father, sitting at the head of the table, was the complete opposite - an old-fashioned Irishman who wouldn't think of coming to dinner without wearing a suit and tie.

After a few nights, Larry told his father that he had to head back to school the next day.

His dad asked, "What time, son?"

"Six o'clock in the morning."

"I'll go with you."

They took the bus and got off at the point where Larry's dad had to say goodbye and return home. As Dad prepared to leave, there were six men standing beneath an awning. Seeing Larry, they started to hurl abuse across the road. They made the sound of a pig and shouted all manner of hurtful comments, including, "If that pig was my kid, I'd hide him in the basement."

As they continued to vilify Larry, his dad did something he had never done before.

He stretched out his arms.

Hugged him.

Kissed him.

And said, "Larry, if your mother and I live to be two hundred years old, that wouldn't be long enough to thank God for the gift he gave us in you. I am so proud that you're my son!"

That was the Christmas present Larry received that year, and it's hard to put into words the lifelong and healing effect it had. He went back to school that day. He cleaned up his appearance the best he could. He even began dating a girl – something he never dreamed he would do. He became president of one of the fraternities. Most spectacular of all, he was the first student in the history of his university to graduate with a 4.2 grade average. It turns out Larry had a brilliant mind. Larry then went on to be ordained a priest and to serve for over two decades as a missionary in South America.

There's no mystery as to why. It was all because his dad, in the face of six bullies, had the courage to gaze at his son's spotty face, see the good in him, and tell him that he loved him.

That's the power of a dad's affirmation right there.

BEWARE OF STEREOTYPES

A lot of the examples in this chapter have circled around a dad's relationship with his son(s). But what about daughters? Do daughters need affirmation in the same way sons do? And do daughters need the same kinds of affirmation?

One of the things I want to say to dads today is, be careful not to create stereotypical and superficial differences between what boys and girls need in the seven dad skills. When it comes to affirmation, you're going to need to start with the uniqueness of your daughter and son, and work from there. Don't start with some preconceived notions about the differences between boys and girls. Let the absolute and priceless individuality of your children set the agenda.

In philosophical terms, what we are talking about here is the difference between a *deductive* and an *inductive* approach to life's questions. In the deductive approach, we start with a general truth, and we work our way down to the particulars to show how they illustrate it. In the inductive approach, we start with the particulars, and we infer general principles and truths from them. The first is a top-down approach. The second is more organic.

Let me give you an example.

Some of the most influential Christian teaching on parenting says that boys have different needs from girls growing up, and vice versa. They claim that a boy's greatest need is for a sense that they are good enough to face the challenges of the world. They want to know that they have what it takes, and they need to have their fathers affirm this. For girls, the theory goes, their needs are different. They need their fathers to tell them that they are beautiful, lovely, gorgeous. While boys want to know that they can fulfil the call to be an adventurous prince, girls want to know they are princesses worth rescuing.

These general truths or principles about boys and girls are widespread, and they have become the basis for the way many fathers exercise the skill of affirmation.

But they are dangerous.

Quite aside from the fact that the Bible itself contains stories of heroic women who do what these teachers claim is restricted to boys (look at Deborah, for one), these kinds of stereotypes keep girls from growing into women who can be leaders in a world that desperately needs to hear their voice and feel their impact. It turns boys into rescuers, girls into damsels in distress. It makes boys active and girls passive. This is not our Heavenly Father's plan.

My advice is this: respect the unique individuality of your daughters, your sons, and work from there. Don't impose a top-down template on them. Tailor your affirmations to their God-given personalities. A daughter who is a bit of a tomboy may not want her father to keep telling her she's beautiful. In fact, it may be the last thing she wants. What she may need is what John Eldredge argues dads should be giving to their boys. He has said this:

"Every little boy growing up has two essential needs from his dad. He needs to know that his dad adores him. He needs to know, 'I love you.' That's core. That comes first. That's the base for everything else. That's the foundation that everything in a boy's life is built upon. "I am the apple of my dad's eye.' He needs to know that.

And he needs to know from his father, "Son, you have what it takes." You see, that's the question every little boy has. 'Do I have what it takes? Will I be a man? Can I come through?' So, through the story of his life, through the tender years, the teenage years, on into young manhood, every man craves this - these two things, love and validation, delight from the father and affirmation."[17]

I agree with what John Eldredge says except this one thing. Those affirmations are what girls need too. If you listen to what Pastor Theresa says at the end of the Dad School video teaching for this session, she says she was looking for her dad to tell her, "you're enough." In other words, "you have what it takes to go conquer the world." Her dad, following the male-versus-female generalisations of his culture, failed to give that to her when she was young. She got it, like many other women, from a spiritual father – Bishop T.D. Jakes. So, the lesson when it comes to the skill of affirmation is this: be very careful not to believe in restrictive male-versus-female distinctions. Start with who your kids are, what your kids need, and work from there. Let them set the agenda, not the limiting beliefs of your religious culture.

REMEMBER WHO YOU ARE!

One of the most striking and memorable examples of the power of affirmation is the Disney animated feature, *The Lion King*. This tells the story of a lion cub called Simba who grows up in the Pride Lands. His father, Mufasa, is the king, and Mufasa mentors Simba in what it means to take his place "in the circle of life."

Mufasa isn't the only older male role model in Simba's life. His uncle – Mufasa's brother – is also around. He's called Uncle Scar. He wants to kill Mufasa so that he and his band of mangy hyenas can rule the Pride Lands. Scar therefore orchestrates a tragic situation in which Mufasa is killed by an army of stampeding wildebeests. Simba, who is with his dad at the time, is devastated. Uncle Scar manages to convince him that it's all his fault that his father has died. Simba, guilty and forlorn, flees from the Pride Lands. He is thoroughly ashamed, and he's now all alone. An outcast. A self-imposed exile. Living far away from home as his wicked Uncle Scar takes Mufasa's throne and leads the Pride Lands into poverty and ruin.

Later in the film, Simba has grown up and is wondering what to do with his life. To cut a long story short, he experiences something of an awakening when he heads out to a pool of water. He stares into it. Looking at the reflection in the stars above, the face of his beloved father Mufasa appears. Mufasa speaks to him, telling him to remember who he is, that he is the King's son, and that he must take his place in the circle of life. When his father disappears, Simba has a new and steely sense of resolve. He will return to the Pride Lands and liberate them from the famine and disaster caused by Scar's selfishness. He will confront and conquer Scar in a final battle to the death. He will bring restoration and abundance to the land his father had ruled.

What an amazing story!

And what a brilliant example of the power of affirmation.

When Simba needs it most, his father affirms him, reminding him who he really is – a royal child. Once he recognises who he really is, Simba understands what he really has. If he's a prince, an heir to the throne, then he possesses royal authority. From this new-found sense of self-worth and significance, Simba seizes his destiny and returns to the Pride Lands to take his rightful place.

Does this remind you of anything?

The father speaking from the heavens?

The affirmation of Simba's sonship?

Of course, it does!

This is Disney's reprise of those moments in the Gospels when the heavens open and Jesus hears the voice of his Heavenly Father reminding him who he is. This scene is a confirmation of how a father's affirmation can release a son or a daughter into their purpose. A father's affirmation is therefore tremendously powerful. It reinforces a sense of identity, and it releases a sense of destiny.

I LOVE ME!

Let's finish where we began, with Marvyn Harrison, and with the problems and solutions he discovered as a dad. The first problem he faced was a generational pattern of absentee fathering. His own father wasn't there for him. He therefore lacked a role model for being a good dad to his two children. We have seen a few times already in this book that this can be a very real disadvantage to fathers, especially fathers of very young children. Marvyn needed to realise that it wasn't his fault that he was incompetent. When he contacted other black dads, he found the same dynamics in the way they saw themselves. They all felt failures because they had been poorly fathered.

The second problem Marvyn faced was the fact that when he was doing his best to father his two kids (both under two), they ran to Mum when he was trying to help them. This just made him feel even more inadequate. Once again, this didn't make him abnormal, nor was it somehow his fault. We have already seen in this book that dads and mums experience different reactions in their brains, and so do their children. Put simply, these reactions cause very young children to run to Mum when they need comforting, and to Dad when they want to play. When Marvyn's son and daughter ran to Mum, this was an entirely natural thing for them to do. It wasn't personal. It was a typical response given the way God the Father has wired not only the brains of fathers and mothers, but children's brains as well.

Marvyn's solution when he heard that all the dads in his group were experiencing this kind of problem was fascinating. He developed the view that his unique role as a father was to use the skill of affirmation. He also made this something that was fun, hence his son laughing when he said, "I am brave!" Marvyn combined the skill of affirmation with the skill of fun.

There was an immediate benefit to his children when he started exercising this skill because they began to believe the title of Marvyn's first book, *I Love Me!*

But there was also a long-term benefit to Marvyn himself. In finding who and what he was, he also discovered his sense of destiny. Consequently, he no longer found himself wondering what his purpose was, or why we are all here. "I've got that glow that I was searching for, that I was missing – and it is really powerful."

Maybe it's time for you to affirm your children.

You'll feel the benefit too as a dad.

QUESTION TIME

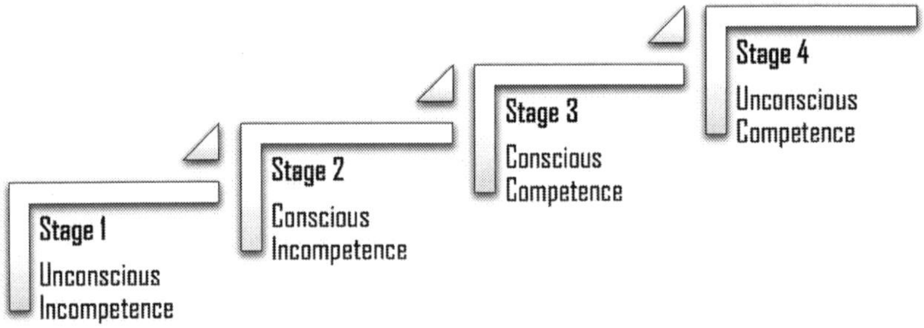

Look at the four stages of learning:
Where are you right now in the skill of giving affirmation?

How are you going to get to the next stage of competence?

What practical changes are you going to make as a dad in the light of what you've just read?

T IS FOR TIME

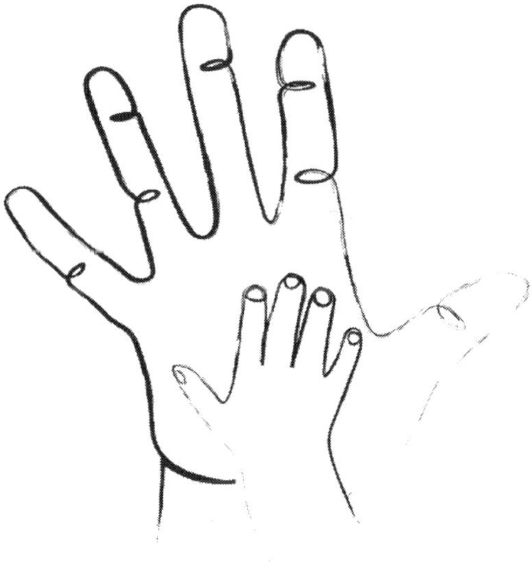

Time is the most valuable coin in your life. You and you alone will determine how that coin will be spent. Be careful that you do not let other people spend it for you.

Carl Sandburg

4
T IS FOR TIME

One of the most memorable conversations I ever had with my father took place when he was suffering from Parkinson's disease. He was concerned about his ailing health and wanted to make the most of the rare moments when I was at home. One day, we sat together in his study in the cellar, surrounded by his books.

"May I ask you a question, my son?"

"Of course, Dad"

"Do you ever think about heaven?"

"Sometimes."

He sighed and said, "I think about it. I think about time, and whether there is any time at all in heaven, or whether time in the way we experience it will be no more."

He looked at me and smiled.

"What do you think?"

"I can tell you what I'd *like* to think."

"Go on."

"What I'd like to think is that eternity, or whatever you want to call it, is a realm that is quite literally timeless. By that I mean, when we find ourselves there, we will not be conscious of the passing of time at all. There will be no sense of looking back at things that happened before, because we won't be aware of *before*..."

"Or *after*," Dad interrupted.

"Precisely. We won't be looking back, and we won't be looking forward, because there will be no consciousness of time having passed, and no sense of time yet to come."

I saw a tear form in Dad's eye.

He took a few seconds before he spoke again and when he did his voice was soft.

He said, "If that is true, and I very much hope that it is, then when I die, I will be in a dimension where I have no awareness of waiting for something in the future. And if we're correct in that view, then I will not have to wait for you to join me..."

I raised my eyebrows, surprised at Dad making such a personal comment, shocked for a moment at his attempt to convey that he did not want to miss me in the hereafter. That was disclosing a level of affection I had not seen before.

"That's what I think too," I said, my voice now as soft as his. "If there's no sense of time passing," I continued, "then you will not be aware of any hours, days, or even years elapsing before we meet again. You will be in a world without time."

Dad said, "Then passing away is the better deal. I will not be conscious of waiting. But you will."

"We all will," I said.

We nodded and got to our feet, Dad a little more tentatively than I had seen before.

He shook my hand, his grip tight, his expression stoical.

"Thank you," he said.

I took my leave and headed upstairs from the cellar to the kitchen where Mum was making lunch.

"Did you have a good chat?" she asked.

"I did."

"And was Dad happy with what you said?"

I nodded.

"I'm so pleased."

I could see the relief in her eyes, and the tiny clouds of grief. When Dad died, I would remember this conversation, as I often have since, and think of him beyond and outside time, waiting without ever being conscious of waiting.

That brings me comfort.

We will be together again in no time at all.

PRESENTS AND PRESENCE

I begin with this story because we now turn to the third skill a dad needs to master and this has to do with time. Dads need to learn that the most important currency they have is not the money they earn from their work but the time they spend with their family. Many fathers fall into the trap of thinking money is more valuable. They may never express it bluntly, but many dads live in a heightened state of busyness, their outward behaviour betraying their inner beliefs. Their value system tells them that they must work all the hours God sends to provide for their children. If this means staying late in the office and missing their child's bedtime, so be it. The higher goal is to provide.

I am not criticizing hard work for one second. Dads should never model laziness to their children. They need to set an example of being conscientious, committed to earning an income through hard graft. Remember, the Bible rails against idleness, especially in the Book of Proverbs where the father figure exhorts his son to avoid being a "sluggard" (the old translation) or a "sleepyhead" (the new). Lazy people fail to do the necessary work of ploughing the fields and sowing the seed. They shouldn't therefore be surprised to find that at harvest there are no crops. They have spent too much time in bed, being indolent instead of industrious. The father who speaks in the Book of Proverbs shows by his own example what he expects from his son.

At the same time, in providing for the family, those of us who are dads need to distinguish between what we think our children need and what our children really need. We also need to take care not to drift from working hard into workaholism.

For example, a father may think their children *need* to have the latest PlayStation or iPhone, and the most expensive holidays to Disney World and the Caribbean. They may even justify this by arguing that not having these material things will cause their son or daughter to be regarded as second-class citizens among their peers. But these are not what children really need. They are what we are tempted to believe they need by all the consumerist messages that bombard us. These messages can drive us into work addiction if we're not careful.

Perhaps my own story will help here.

When, in 1996, I became the senior leader of a large church in the UK, I became aware of how wealthy nearly everyone was in my parish. My mother had warned me about this. She called the community as a "gin and jag belt." In other words, it was the kind of place where people drove Jaguars and drank a lot of cocktails.

It turned out she was right.

Bringing my four children up in this culture was not easy. Their friends had all they wanted and went on frequent holidays. I was earning a very small salary and looking to charities for the money just to clothe and feed my children. What was I to do?

I decided to start accepting invitations to travel the world and speak at prestigious and popular conferences. I also accepted commissions from publishers who were chasing me to accept book deals. This did two things: it brought in enough extra money to give my children the toys and treats their friends had, but it also meant that I was frequently away. When I did come home, I was trying to lead one of the largest churches in the country, sustain a career as a popular writer, and keep accepting invitations as an in-demand speaker. This took its toll. I was permanently jet-lagged and fatigued. More importantly, it gave me little time for my children. What time I did have, I spent poorly. I was so emotionally depleted that I couldn't be empathetically engaged with them. I failed them as a father.

What was I doing wrong? I was providing for my family, after all. What could be more important than that? I'll tell you. Children may *want* our ***presents***, but they *need* our ***presence***. If you and I believe that money is the most important currency, we will not understand this. We need to come to realise that time is the most precious thing we have. Nothing is more important than spending quality time with our children. Exercising the skill of time is a top priority in our lives. Once that time has gone, we won't get it back again. As someone once said, "No man ever said on his deathbed, 'I wish I'd spent more time at the office'." He's right. No one in history has ever said that. I just wish I'd realised this when my kids were going through the teenage years. You can get your money back, but not your time.

HOOKED BY WORK

I used to take my children to the cinema many times when they were young. One of those family outings was to see the Steven Spielberg feature, *Hook*, starring Robin Williams and Dustin Hoffman (1991). Being fans of pirate stories, it was a no-brainer. Williams plays Peter Banning, a workaholic businessman who is putting his job before his two young children (a son and a daughter). Peter Banning was once Peter Pan when he was a boy. As an adult, he's lost his childlike spirit of play and adventure. Even at his son's school play, he's talking to his business partner on his mobile phone.

Peter's wife Moira (Caroline Goodall) watches on until one day they pay a family visit to the house in London where Peter had once lived. They arrive tired and jet-lagged from the States. Peter gets on his phone straightaway to help orchestrate a deal. When he's finished, Moira takes him on one side and tells him some home truths.

"Your children love you. They want to play with you. How long do you think that lasts? Soon Jack [your son] may not even want you to come to his games.

We have a few special years with our children when they're the ones who want us around. After that you're going to be running after them for a bit of attention.

It's so fast, Peter.

It's a few years and then it's over.

You are not being careful, and you are missing it."

That's some speech, and it sets the tone for the rest of the film. Peter is running out of time. Only when his children are abducted and taken to Neverland does he start to realise it. When they fall foul of Captain Hook (Dustin Hoffman), Peter reacts. He heads there himself and confronts his archenemy.

In many ways, Hook was a warning to me – both Hook the man and *Hook* the movie. Hook lives in constant fear of being swallowed up by a great crocodile – a crocodile whose presence is indicated by the ominous ticking of a clock. Hook is a man surrounded by clocks. He has destroyed all their mechanisms so they cannot tick. What is all this if it's not a great fear connected with time? This is what Peter is in danger of becoming. He's been devoured by the endless ticking of a clock. He's become obsessed with getting his work done on time. In the process, he's lost sight of who he really is – Peter Pan! To rescue his children, and indeed himself, he must rediscover the light side of his character – the childlike love of play, fun, games, and adventure. Only when he does this will he become fully human and fully alive again. Only when he puts first things first will he become the father his children need him to be. Spielberg was warning me. I didn't listen.

ABOUT TIME

One person who got things right was the father in the famous story Jesus told in Luke 15 – a passage of Scripture that has formed the foundation for the views about fatherhood in this book. In Luke 15, when the rebellious boy runs away from home, taking his financial inheritance with him, the father spends many months and possibly years watching and waiting for his son to return home. Then, when he sees the silhouette of his boy on the desert horizon, he runs to him and envelops him in his arms. As a feast is held in honour of his homecoming, the boy's older brother complains about the extravagance. The father takes the trouble to explain to him that every good thing the boy has ever wanted he could have asked for and received. All he had to do was come to his dad and make the request. If he had wanted a party for 200 people – a party with an outdoor barbeque with prime beef roasting on a spit – then he could have had that too.

What we see here is a father who has mastered the skill of time. On two occasions on the same day, this dad goes out to each of his sons and engages with them at the deepest level. This is what in *Dad School* we mean by the skill of time. The skill of time involves two things. It firstly involves a father being *physically present* to his child. We're not saying that a zoom call or a phone conversation is without any merit or value. These can still be helpful if that's all we can do. But a dad being present in a physical way allows for demonstrations of affection that are simply not possible when communicating via a tablet or a smartphone. Physical presence allows you to do what the dad does in Luke 15 – to express your love for your child with a hug or a kiss.

Physical presence on its own is not enough, however. A dad can be present in body but not in spirit, after all. Put another way, he can be physically present but emotionally absent. So, the second aspect of the skill of time is empathetic or *emotional engagement*. It involves listening to what your child is trying to communicate, hearing it, feeling it, and demonstrating that you understand what they're telling you. Remember, the father in Luke 15 is extremely emotionally engaged. When he sees his son returning from the far country, Jesus says that this dad was "moved with compassion." That's a rather lame translation. The original Greek word contains the word for "guts." This was *visceral* empathy. The dad was torn apart by the sight of his returning boy.

Exercising the skill of time therefore involves both physical presence and emotional engagement:

The parable Jesus composed portrays a loving father who clearly understood that his relationship with his two sons superseded every other priority in his life. In this respect, we can say of him that he is the most invested of all fathers. He understood the importance of giving time to both his sons, and he also understood that this required him to go to both his boys and to be with them physically. Equally important, he realized that in both cases what they needed was undiminished emotional engagement and empathetic listening. To quote the title of a Richard Curtis movie (one that also focuses on a father-son relationship), the entire story is *About Time*.

KAIROS DADS

One of the best ways dads can learn how to master this temporal skill is by learning about the two different types of time. In English, we only have one word for time, but the New Testament part of the Bible was originally written in a popular, marketplace kind of Greek. In this ancient language, there were two words for time.

The first word often translated "time" in the New Testament is the Greek word *chronos*, from which we get *chronology*. As you can probably guess, this kind of time is the ordinary, mundane, often tedious progression of time. Think of Peter Banning in *Hook*. He lives by the clock and will, if he doesn't mend his ways, end up dying by the clock, which is exactly what happens to Captain Hook. The enormous quantity of clocks in Captain Hook's pirate ship just proves the point. *Chronos* is characterised by the unstoppable ticking of the clock. It establishes when you are meant to get up, when you are meant to go to work, when you are meant to eat, when you are meant to come home, when you are meant to go to sleep. *Chronos* rules our lives. Like Peter Banning, our daily routines are accompanied and dominated by *chronos*. We are creatures that mark out our lives *chronologically*.

The second word often translated "time" is the Greek word *kairos*. This is a different kind of time. If *chronos* is ordinary, mundane, finite time, *kairos* is the opposite. It is a kind of time that is extraordinary, special, infinite in quality. When Jesus emerges from his season of great preparation, he begins his three-year public ministry with the words, "the time has been fulfilled." The word translated "time" here is not *chronos*, it's *kairos*. This kind of time refers to exceptional and unique moments in history. It refers to those moments in which God the Father intervenes within our chronological time to do something of infinite importance – such as the birth of his Son, or the start of his Son's ministry. These are examples of *kairos*. When it comes to *kairos*, the opportunity of a lifetime must be seized within the lifetime of that opportunity. The two words therefore have different connotations. Although we should be careful not to overstate the differences, *chronos* is about the quantity of time, *kairos* the quality of time.

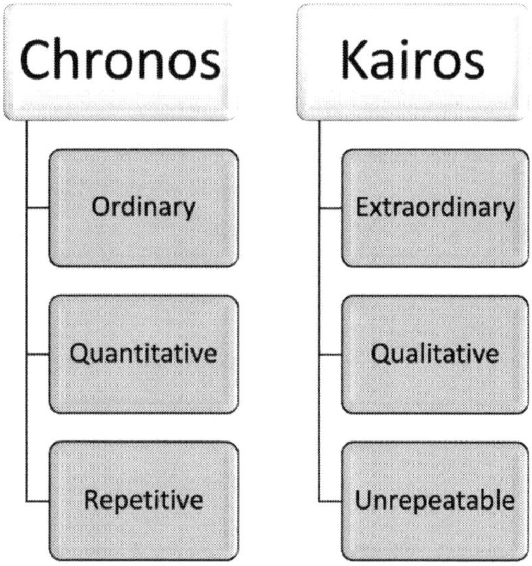

MOST WONDERFUL DAYS

Any father who wants to master the skill of time must become wise about these two dimensions of time. One of the things we now know from countless studies of fatherhood is that what a child remembers most is not so much the quantity of time that a dad spends with them as it is its quality. Dads who master the skill of time make sure that the time they invest is more about *kairos* than *chronos*. Some fathers are legitimately busy, as mine was. My dad was the headteacher of a large school in Norwich, North Norfolk. He rarely came home before seven o'clock at night and was often away to work before I had a chance to see him at breakfast. Yet I remember precious moments when he was both physically present and emotionally engaged with me. I cherish memories of him just being there – being there in both senses (being present and being attentive). I am truly grateful.

At *Dad School*, we teach that fathers need honestly to admit that from their perspective the time they spend with their kids can sometimes feel to them like it's *chronos* – ordinary, sometimes tedious, often repetitive time. But they also need to see that from their child's point of view, when they are physically present and emotionally engaged, that's *kairos* - extraordinary, special, history-making experiences. They are like those *kairos* moments described in the Bible when our Father in Heaven acted in a once-in-a-lifetime way. They are moments heavy-laden with significance and destiny. They are *kairos*.

There's a well-known story about a man called Charles Francis Adams, son of US President John Adams. Charles Francis Adams went on to become the U.S. diplomat to Great Britain. You could say he became a very busy man with a lot of very important responsibilities. Yet he is not remembered primarily for his achievements in the workplace so much as his failures at home.

One incident stands out above them all.

One day, he decided to go out fishing with his son, Brook Adams. He wrote an entry in his journal which may rank among some of the worst things a dad has ever said.

"Went fishing with my son today."

He summarised the experience thus.

"A day wasted."

His son Brook also kept a diary.

"Went fishing with my father," he wrote.

His summary?

"The most wonderful day of my life."

Perhaps no other story about fathers showcases the point I'm making here. From a father's perspective, the time they invest in interacting with their children may sometimes feel repetitive and mundane. It may, in short, feel like *chronos*. But I can guarantee that from the child's perspective, it can feel the opposite. It may, in short, feel like *kairos* – the most wonderful day of their lives.

My advice is this: see every moment with your child as *kairos*. Make it quality time.

LEARNING FROM FAILURE

It's at this point I have become very aware that I'm at risk of violating my own principles and making out as if (a) I am the ultimate fatherhood guru, and (b) I am a total success as a dad. If I'm implying either of these things, I apologise. The truth is, I've sometimes made mistakes when it comes to exercising the skill of time.

During the time when I was effectively doing three jobs (leading a church, speaking at conferences, writing books), one of my children came to me. We shared a mutual interest in all things World War 2. Still do. The child in question was about thirteen.

"Dad, can we go to the WW2 exhibition at the air museum near Cambridge – the one we often drive past?"

"Of course."

I asked my P.A. to find a date.

When the day came, I had just returned from a preaching trip in the USA and was not sleeping well. I was also suffering some severe work-related stress. My marriage was under immense strain. I was not, as the saying goes, "all there."

We drove for two hours and headed into the museum. I don't remember anything about the tour around the WW2 hangers, except that I was not embracing and living in the moment and was in a hurry to get to the exit and come home.

On the way back, my child broke the silence that had accompanied almost the entire experience.

"Are you okay, Dad?"

I was shocked by the question.

"Why do you ask?"

"Because you've hardly said anything to me all day."

I remember the feeling of shame that crept through my body like hemlock. There was no denying it. I had been very quiet. I had not been emotionally disengaged when it was needed most.

Many years later, my life would implode under the pressures I had been carrying, including my own flaws. I went through two years of counselling and restoration. This included facing up to the terrible feelings of abandonment I'd experienced when I had been left behind at a boarding school on my eighth birthday. I was severely beaten by a teacher that first night. Under my bedsheets, I made a vow: if I was going to get through the next ten years boarding, I was going to have to remove my emotion chip and stop feeling.

So, that's what I did.

And I never put it back in again.

Not until my two years of counselling.

A few years after that, the child I had wounded was now an adult going through mental health problems. We spoke almost every day. Sometimes two to three times a day. We met frequently. During those times, I was not just physically present, I was completely engaged emotionally. Those conversations proved to be quite literally lifesaving. In one of them, I apologised from the heart for the day out at the WW2 air museum. My beautiful child forgave me. God forgave me. And in the end, I even managed to forgive myself.

Today, God is restoring the years the locusts have eaten.

He's good at that.

He's the Perfect Dad.

IT'S TIME TO WISE UP!

In Ephesians 5:15-16, the Apostle Paul wrote, "Be careful then how you live, not as unwise people but as wise, making the most of the time." If there's a word for dads, it's right there. Dads need to exercise wisdom when it comes to time, and there are two areas I'd like to emphasize where the need for wisdom is pressing.

The first is at the personal level. Individual dads need to exercise wisdom in the way they spend time with their children. At this point, I'm not so much talking about *when* as *how*. I'm going to take it as read that you and I recognize it is important to decide on the *when*. We need to carve out spaces on a regular basis for investing in quality time – in *kairos* time – with our children. It's *how* we set up that time and *how* we spend it that I'm concerned about. Some fathers may need to wise up in the way they do these things. And top of my list of concerns is the so-called Daddy-Daughter Date.

I'm not questioning whether dads should spend quality time with their daughters. They should. And they should do the same with their sons. But what I am questioning is whether dads should use the word "date" when doing this. The only date dad should be having is with Mum. If you call these outings with your daughter a "date," you're using a romantic metaphor. Romanticizing your relationship with your daughter is not healthy. It is sending the wrong signals. Please just consider being consistent here: call it Father-Daughter *Time*, just as you would call it Father-Son *Time*. Be wise here. If a mother took her son out to MacDonalds and called it a Mummy-Son Date, every Freudian psychoanalyst in the country would rightly be up in arms. As dads, let's be wise at the personal level.

And let's be wise at a societal level too. It is shocking just how little value is placed in society on a father's right to be with their child not only when they are born, but in the years that follow. Over the last 100 years or so, dads have been increasingly pushed to the margins when it comes to parenting. Their role has been less and less honoured and more and more devalued. Governments don't seem to care whether fathers have quality time with their children. They do not develop either planning or policies to support dads.

There are two nations that prove to be the exception to this rule. Norway's government has historically maintained a very generous plan and policy when it comes to paternity leave - 15 weeks of non-transferable, use-it-or-lose-it paid leave. Then there's the Netherlands. They encourage new dads to take "daddy days" (*papadag*). In 2016, nearly 50% of young fathers in the Netherlands took a day off at least once a week to be at home with their child - a percentage that has continued to increase. How's your nation doing? Does it recognize the inestimable value of invested fathers?

It's time for dads to be wise about how they use their time. We need to be wise about how we enjoy quality time with our sons and daughters. And we need to be wise in the way we encourage governments to release more resources for dads to spend that time, especially when their children are born.

The good news is this. It seems the tide is beginning to turn. Studies over the last ten years or so have confirmed that fathers are of vital and primary importance in the raising of children. Scripture has told us this for two thousand plus years. Now the science is reinforcing it. The data tells us this is so. Dr Anna Machin – the leading expert on the science of fatherhood – says that the current focus on the culture of fathering is not just a passing academic fad. She argues that there is real societal change happening. In the UK, the science is telling us what some of us have always known from Scripture, that dads are special and unique. This is therefore a moment of opportunity. It is a *kairos* time for dads to lobby for *kairos* time.

LOCKDOWN DADS

Perhaps nothing illustrates this more compellingly than the way the global pandemic challenged many fathers with respect to their priorities. During the lockdowns in 2020-21, many fathers found themselves for the first time working from home (WFH). This created a paradigm shift in their thinking. The amount of time they spent with their children doubled overnight, and their awareness of what their stay-at-home spouse or partner invested in their children was enhanced. The Fatherhood Institute, seeing this play out, decided to take advantage of what was a unique social experiment. Recognizing that this was what we would call a *kairos* moment, they seized the opportunity of a lifetime within the lifetime of the opportunity. They conducted their own research project into lockdown dads.[18]

The results were startling. The Fatherhood Institute already knew that 150 years ago the Industrial Revolution had removed many dads from the home. No longer working in the fields nearby, men spent hours travelling to the local coalmines. There they spent long and arduous hours digging for coal. They would return late to their families, often covered in soot, always exhausted. In the process, they became less and less involved in hands-on fathering within the home.

In 2020 this historical pattern was reversed. Governments mandated that people were now to stay at home and isolate themselves. What this did for fatherhood was nothing short of seismic. When the Fatherhood Institute research team interviewed many of the new stay-at-home dads, they discovered that these men had:

- Come to see the importance of time with their children
- Spent more time with their children
- Felt much closer to their children
- Grown more confident as fathers
- Gained greater insight into their wife's/partner's role
- Played a fuller part in their children's education
- Decided they wanted more flexible working patterns

As one father put it, "After work I used to be knackered... Just wanted to get home and put the TV on. Now I can actually spend time with my son and feel awake."

As a result of these findings, the Fatherhood Institute has been encouraging employers to support more flexible working patterns for men. They have also asked the UK government to legislate for employers to detail flexibility options in job advertisements, and to provide reports annually on how well they are doing. The Fatherhood Institute should be applauded. They have been helping dads to exercise the skill of time at home with their children.

NO MORE STILL FACES

This is a good moment in history for dads to be prioritizing the time they spend with their children. As we have seen in this chapter, this investment of time is not just a matter of being physically present; it's also a matter of being emotionally engaged. I shared right at the beginning how my own adoptive father may not have spent a lot of time with me (*chronos*), but what time he did spend was meaningful and memorable (*kairos*). I then confessed that I did not always follow his good example. I made mistakes. On at least one occasion, I was physically present to my teenage child, but I was emotionally absent. At a crucial age, when they needed my empathy, I was, as my Northern Irish wife would put it, "away in the head."

There are three main reasons why fathers and father figures should learn to invest in *kairos* time with their children.

The first is Scriptural.

The sacred Scriptures show fathers how to exercise the skill of time. We saw this in the father in Luke 15. He was an expert in the skill of time. He invested time in both his sons on the same day. He was present to them in person, and he was empathetic to their needs. He was truly an invested dad.

The second is societal.

The great social changes and upheavals of the last few years have brought about a new awareness in fathers of the importance of undoing some of the damage done by the Industrial Revolution. As the Fatherhood Institute put it, at the start of the first lockdown in 2020 millions of fathers started coming home again. This has created an irreversible and indelible sea change in the way many fathers view their priorities. As dads, we now place a supreme value in spending quality time with our kids. The WFH revolution has truly begun.

The third is scientific.

The new science of fatherhood is simply underlining the Scriptural and societal truths we've come to know. Dads are special and unique. They have a vital place in the home. When dads are not present to their children, for whatever reason, not only do their children suffer adverse consequences. Society suffers as well. But when dads are physically present and emotionally engaged with their children, the scientific data confirms that there are health benefits all around. Children develop in more positive directions. The foundations of society are greatly strengthened in the process.

If you still have problems understanding the importance of this new science of fatherhood, just type Still Face with Dads into your YouTube search engine. You'll see young fathers conducting what's called the still-face experiment with their infant children. When these dads are physically present and emotionally engaged, father and child play together comfortably. They are completely attuned to each other. When these dads are asked by the researchers to turn their faces away, then turn back but look away from their child, with a "still face," the results are immediate and devastating. Within three minutes, the baby has dissolved into discomfort, crying, despair. When dad is told to turn back and reengage in play, the baby settles down straightaway and nestles back into their comfort zone with Dad.

This research is based on the famous Still Face Experiment created by Dr Ed Tronick which revealed that this initial interaction between father and child is key to the baby's success in growing up as a child, especially in their ability to trust others, to explore the world, and keep on an even keel. But the research also provokes a disturbing question. What will life be like for babies whose constant experience is like those three minutes of disengagement all the time?

Dads need to invest *kairos* times with their children right from the beginning. There are Scriptural, societal, and now scientific reasons for making this a priority.

Literally everyone benefits.

A FIELD OF DREAMS

I return now to where I began, with my adoptive father talking to me about time, and the two of us speculating what time will feel like for us in the hereafter, in eternity. That conversation was a *kairos* moment with my father. It was unique. Special. Intense. Loving. Unforgettable. And I hope one day we will both be able to meet again and discover that our bold philosophising is true.

In the meantime, I miss these moments terribly. How I've longed to be able to pick up the phone and just talk to him again? How I have missed those visits when I could enjoy his presence, bask in the glow of that warm smile of his, and revel in the pride that shone so brightly from his dark eyes. When I was walking through a valley of many shadows ten years ago, I would have done anything to be able to hear his soothing voice and listen to his reassuring wisdom – a wisdom forged on the anvil of great suffering.

I don't think I'm alone in feeling these things.

Many of us long for more time with dad.

Perhaps no film has explored this longing more powerfully than the classic *Field of Dreams*. Kevin Costner's character (Ray Kinsella) is troubled by the fact that he never really knew his dad. His dad (John Kinsella) was too busy playing baseball. When Ray builds a baseball field, the ghost of his dad appears, young and dressed in a baseball outfit. The two spend time together talking and playing catch. The lack that Ray has felt since his childhood is healed. It is a touch of heaven, as both father and son come to agree.

If you watch the scene again on YouTube (Field of Dreams – Playing Catch), read some of the responses written by people in the comments section, especially those by people who have lost their dads and long for just one more game of catch.

Three stand out for me.

May they inspire all dads to exercise the skill of time.

"This scene reminds me of having a catch with my dad," the first writes. "He always found time for me, no matter how busy he was at work. He was always at all my sporting events growing up, and it taught me to believe in myself."

They conclude, "I miss you, dad and love you with all my heart. I can't wait to have our next catch when I see you again."

The second comment is even more poignant.

"My dad and I used to play catch every day in the front yard. In two days, it'll be nine years since he passed away. Every year I go to his gravesite and leave a baseball on his tombstone. I cry every time I watch this scene."

The third is truly heart-breaking.

"I remember how much this scene affected my father when he saw it. He lost his father at 15, his father was 46. It affects me now, having lost my father at 18, when he was 47. I would give anything to have another day with him."

QUESTION TIME

Look at the four stages of learning:

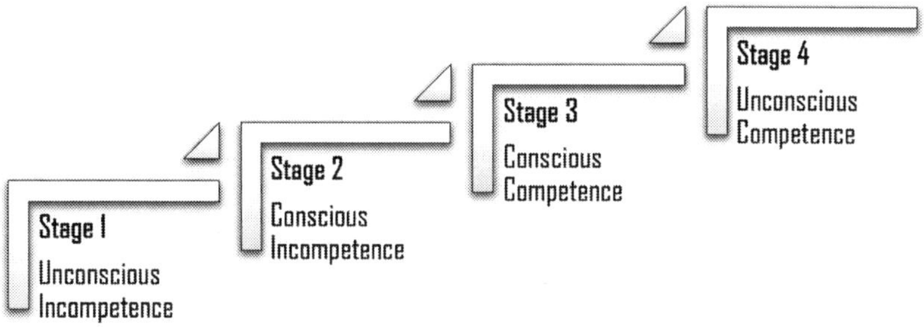

Where are you right now in the skill of investing in quality time?

How are you going to get to the next stage of competence?

What practical changes are you going to make as a dad in the light of what you've just read?

H IS FOR HUGS

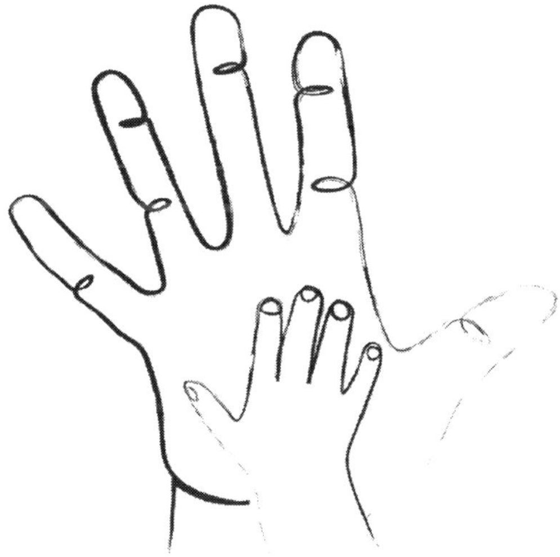

My father, there was never any mistaking his love for me. When I walked into the room, his eyes lit up and he wrapped me in his arms as if it was Christmas morning and I was the best gift imaginable!

Eric Ripert

5
H IS FOR HUGS

You've probably been living under a rock if you haven't heard of the fallout between Prince Harry and the British royal family. All families have their occasional spats, but most keep these within the confines of the home. Not so Prince Harry. He and his wife Meghan Markel have been interviewed by Oprah Winfrey, featured in a Netflix series, and produced a bestselling book, all of which have given them a very public opportunity to air their grievances. The title of the book, *Spare*, will probably give you a clue as to what these resentments are. Prince Harry's experience of living in the royal household mirrored his mother's. He feels like he has been an outsider, insignificant, surplus to requirements. The only person that could heal that wound was King Charles, but Harry claims he missed out on his father's love. His father didn't give him the affection and support he needed.

Yesterday, my smartphone issued a news alert. It was a headline piece about a new claim made by Prince Harry that his father never hugged him. This lack made Prince Harry more determined than ever to father his own children well. In the news item, he said he now smothers his own children with physical affection to make sure he doesn't pass on the trauma of not being hugged.

Being an investigative journalist, the writer of this report considered two questions. The first, what constitutes a hug? The answer, *to hold someone close to your body with your arms, usually to show that you like, love, or value them*. The second, was Harry as deprived as he claims? There then followed photos of Charles holding Harry as a little boy, Charles breaking from a game of polo to show affection for his son (this was followed by two more polo-related photos of his dad hugging him), a hug by his dad on a ski trip, a hug and a kiss on the tenth anniversary of Diana's death, and a warm embrace by his dad at the Chelsea Flower Show a few years later.[19]

The photographic evidence reveals that Prince Harry did experience physical affection from his father. Why then does Harry argue otherwise? What he may be saying is that his father didn't hug him in private, away from the cameras. Where it mattered – behind closed doors – his father was not demonstrative. This was important, no *traumatic*, for Harry not just because his mother was now dead, but because the young prince understood that his father's hug provided something precious, comforting, reassuring, even healing. He is not wrong in believing this. There is something unique about a father's hug – something that confers the kind of benefits that even a mother's embrace cannot supply in the same way or measure. As Scripture and science show, there is something very significant about a dad's embrace. Its positive effects can last a lifetime.

FOUR TYPES OF CONTACT

It's interesting at this point to think about the way men hug. If you're anything like me, you will have seen at least three toned-down versions of a full-on hug. Let's consider three.

There is, firstly, the **handshake**. The handshake is the least impactful expression of physical affection. I remember one time being in Norwich Cathedral worshipping at a communion service. Just before the breaking of the bread, everyone in the congregation was encouraged to offer one another a sign of the peace of Christ. I turned to see who I could hug. The first person in my eyeline was one of those very well-spoken, elderly British gentlemen – a man with the silvery hair and silky elocution of Charles Dance. He was probably a retired British Army colonel. When I lunged towards him, he reached out his hand with great reluctance, not only to halt my advance (further proof that he was a military man), but to shake mine in what was the bare minimum requirement when it came to giving a sign of the peace. As he did so, he said in an impeccable English accent, and with the air of a true aristocrat, "Oh, very well. If you must."

The handshake is perhaps the lowest form of hug. It is the last resort of those who would, if they could, make all PDAs (public demonstrations of affection) illegal!

Then, secondly, there's the crab option - **the sideways hug**. You've probably seen this. Maybe you've even done it. My brother is an expert at this kind of gesture. He won't risk the full-on frontal hug with me; he will either shake my hand when saying hello (or goodbye), or he will – if he's feeling this way inclined – put his arm around my shoulder. This protects him against a chest-to-chest form of physical contact (God forbid!), but it allows him at least some semblance of physical contact beyond the simple shaking of hands.

Thirdly, there's **the pat on the back**. This is when a man will hug another man, or his older child, and pat their shoulder three times with their hand or fingers. When the third pat is over, the two will release each other from this rather awkward display of affection. The third is a kind of code - an unspoken, unwritten social contract. It's a signal that this has now got to stop.

There are many men like this. Their theme song is not, "Knock three times," but "Pat three times." Theirs is not a full hug. It's a kind of "Well done" more than an "I love you."

There are therefore three lesser versions of hugging. Leading up to the fourth and fullest expression – **holding someone close to your body with your arms** – there's the handshake, the side hug, and the pat on the back. If we're being fair to Prince Harry, few of the photos of his dad reveal the fourth and fullest expression. They are all the lesser, more Stoical versions – especially the side hug.

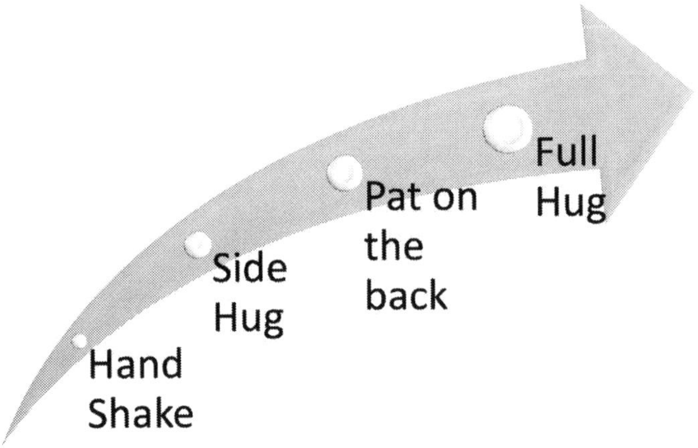

A FATHER'S EMBRACE

The bedrock for the seven father skills in this book is the story told by Jesus in chapter 15 of Luke's Gospel. This should not be called the Parable of the Prodigal Son because the hero of the story is not the son at all. It's the father. A better title is the Parable of the Extravagantly Loving Father. This father displays far more love than any Jewish dad at the time would have been expected to show.

At the critical point in the story, he sees his son returning home. The boy is emaciated and broke. He stinks of the pigpen. What happens next is very telling. This is my amplified translation.

When his father caught sight of him, he was filled with a gut-wrenching pity. Seized by a great affection, the father ran like the wind towards his son.

As soon as he got to him, the father fell upon the boy's drooping and dirty shoulders, hugging him without a care for what any of the villagers thought of him.

Then, having loosed him from his arms, the father looked at his beloved son's face.

Overcome with joy, he kissed him.

Not just once.

But over and over.

Never saying a word.

I think you'd call that a PDA!

Let me tell you why I have translated the original Greek version of the episode like this. Some English translations say that the father "embraced" the boy. But the original word is *pipto*, which means literally that he fell upon his son's shoulders or threw his arms around his boy's neck. That's altogether more demonstrative and affectionate. It's a very physical and poignant gesture.

Then there's the word kiss. Most translations say that the father "kissed" his son. But the verb has both a continuous and an intensive connotation. This means that the father kissed his boy fervently and repeatedly. Hence my translation.

So, let me put it plainly.

This is not a handshake.

It is not a side hug.

It is not a pat on the back.

It is a full-on, unrestrained hug.

What a beautiful picture.

And what a timeless example.

THE WEEPING SHARK

When we see this father's very public demonstration of affection, we cannot help thinking of our own fathers. This dad sets the bar when it comes to hugging. It's hard to imagine any man being more unashamedly demonstrative. Yet many of us have had fathers who were simply not willing or capable of hugging us in this way. Maybe they were not hugged by their own dads. Maybe this is a perpetuation of a cultural or generational deficit.

In 1996, golfer Greg Norman had a nightmare final round at the Masters. Norman, whose nickname was 'The Shark', was within sight of his first Green Jacket but threw it all away with a round of 78. He had started the day with a six-shot lead over England's Nick Faldo, aka 'The Iceman.' By the end of that same day, he was five strokes behind Faldo. Faldo's round of 67 gave him a five-shot victory.

What happened next is one of the most memorable and moving moments in golfing history. On the 18th green, Faldo walked towards his rival. He held himself back from over-celebrating even though he had just executed a 15-foot Birdie putt.

Norman tried to smile but couldn't. He had just blown a big lead and lost the tournament.

What happened next shocked Norman. Faldo enveloped him in a huge embrace, consoling his defeated rival in a stunning display of sportsmanship. The world watched on in amazement as the Iceman and the Shark hugged each other. Many could see that Norman was deeply moved. Some observed that he was in tears.

Later, in December of that same year, Norman reflected on why this hug had touched him so deeply. He shared memories of his childhood, and especially of how emotionally disengaged his dad was whenever he returned from work trips.

"I used to see my father, getting off a plane or something, and I'd want to hug him, but he would only shake my hand."

Norman was then asked why he was in tears when Faldo embraced him. He replied that it wasn't because he had lost. He'd lost before, and he said he would lose again. Then he explained.

"I cried because I'd never felt that from another man before. I've never had a hug like that in my life."

I don't know about you, but that's one of the saddest things I've ever heard. No child should ever be allowed to grow up without experiencing regular daddy hugs. Even if these hugs are from stand-in fathers or father figures, no child should be robbed of the reassuring embrace of an older, loving, male role model. That Greg Norman was only allowed a handshake from his father is so tragic. What a huge deficit this produced in his life.

This story is a telling and timely reminder to all dads to develop the skill of hugging. Not handshakes, side hugs, or pats on the back. I'm talking about proper hugs. Given in the right way at the right time, a father's embrace can be lifechanging.

MAKING UP THE HUG DEFICIT

What hope is there for someone like Greg Norman, and the many like him? How can a grown man be healed of the hug deficit left by an emotionally repressed dad?

Here I make no apologies for providing a faith-based solution. My experience of thirty years of helping people with father wounds has taught me one great truth. Put generally, this is that there can be miracles when we believe, as the song in *The Prince of Egypt* reminds us. Put more specifically, it is that the healing love of God the Father can make up the hug deficit in our hearts.

All this is supported by both Scripture and experience. In the Scriptures, God makes a wonderful promise to all those with abandonment issues caused by their parents. King David, in Psalm 27:10, sang this great truth: "Even though my father and my mother may abandon me, the Lord will hold me close."

Let's unpack this.

In this great verse, God tells us that he is acutely aware of the traumatic wounds that our parents may inflict, including the wound of abandonment. God is not an aloof Father. He is an invested Father. He is emotionally engaged with us in our pain. He feels what we feel. He is God with us – the empathetic Dad.

When we bring the wounds from our fathers to this perfect

Father, not only are we met with understanding. We also encounter healing. How does this happen? Psalm 27:10 tells us. If we have missed out on a father's embrace (maybe because he was physically or emotionally absent), our Heavenly Father will make up the deficit. How? By holding us close. Does this mean that our Father who is in heaven hugs his children while they are here on earth?

Yes, it does!

Put briefly, the bad news is that many adults have a hug deficit from their earthly parents. God knows and acknowledges that our dads let us down, as even our mothers can too.

The good news is that God also promises that when we have missed out on earthly hugs, there are heavenly hugs available to us. The father of the prodigal son assures us this is so. The whole point of the story is that this affectionate father is a portrait of God the Father – the world's greatest Dad. The listeners to this story have been painting God out to be aloof and angry. Jesus provides the antidote to this toxic image of God. He provides a radical picture of God as the Father who, in Jesus, runs to us and embraces us.

BOBBY'S CRY

Psalm 27 verse 10 teaches us that our Heavenly Father can and will make up the hug deficit when we believe in him. And this is also borne out by experience. Although everyone is unique, and God's ways are both marvellous and mysterious, what I can say is that he comes to us as we are when we ask him to, and he envelops us in his arms of love if we are desperate for his embrace.

How does he do this? By his Holy Spirit. In the Bible, the premier ministry or role of the Holy Spirit is to assure us that we are the adopted children of God. That this knowledge is experiential not just intellectual is beyond any reasonable doubt. Listen to how the Apostle Paul describes the work of this same Holy Spirit in Romans 8:15:

"The Spirit you received does not make you slaves, so that you live in fear again; rather, the Spirit you received brought about your adoption to sonship. And by him we cry, '*Abba*, Father'."

That this is an emotional rather than a purely theological gift is confirmed by the word *cry*. We cry "Daddy" when we are filled with the Spirit of adoption. It's heartfelt.

If you want a picture in literature of what this feels and looks like in real life, remember the conclusion to E.E. Nesbitt's classic children's story, *The Railway Children*. There, a father is wrongfully arrested and removed from his family. His wife and three children leave their home and go to live in the country. Every day the children rush outside to the railway and wave at the train that stops at their local railway station. They long to see their father again. They hope that someday one of these old locomotives will bring him home.

Then, one day, it happens.

Bobby, the wronged man's daughter, is waiting on the platform as an old steam engine pulls into the station. Passengers alight from the carriages. They step onto the platform and walk out of the station, travelling on to their next destination.

Bobby waits.

There is a great cloud of steam at the end of the train as she continues to stare down the line.

She peers into the mist.

Then she sees it.

The outline of a man.

Tall.

Distinguished.

Dark cloak.

Briefcase.

He starts to walk towards her.

She recognises him.

And she utters one of the greatest and most heart-breaking lines in literature (and film).

"Daddy! Oh, my Daddy!"

It is a beautiful homecoming.

That's the kind of thing I'm talking about. Bobby *cried* "Daddy!" You can only *cry* the word Daddy if you've first felt the deepest possible longing for something.

What is that?

A hug from your father.

The Holy Spirit can give that to you.

SID'S STORY

There are so many stories I could tell at this point but let me just share one. In the days when I was travelling a lot, sharing the message of the Father's love, I spoke at a conference in Canada. I was asked to give a talk at an evening session. While I was speaking, I saw a man sitting on his own with his head in his hands. He looked desperate, but because he was quite a way away in the far corner of the conference hall, I couldn't see exactly what was happening to him.

When I reached the end of my talk, I invited all those who wanted to experience their Heavenly Father's love to come forward to the stage. I asked them to stand with their hands outstretched in front, in an attitude of faith, expecting to receive.

I watched as the man in the far corner walked to the front. He didn't seem to know what to do. Instead of standing facing me, he sat down with his back to the stage.

He was clearly very deeply moved.

After a while, as members of the local ministry team started praying for people, I went and sat next to him.

"What's your name?" I asked.

"Sid."

"What's happening, Sid?"

"Something while you were speaking."

I waited for him to explain.

"I was sitting alone because I didn't want to be near anyone else. I was listening to you talking about this perfect Heavenly Father. All I could think about was my own dad. He died when I was five years old. That was sixty years ago."

"I'm sorry," I said.

Sid continued. "I put my head in my hands and closed my eyes. As I did, I felt these strong arms around me. I opened my eyes. There was no one there."

I smiled.

"I did this twice more. Same thing happened. Then, after the third hug, I began to understand what was happening. God was holding me. It felt so strong. So, reassuring. I haven't felt that for sixty years. It was amazing. I feel completely different."

He stood.

"You know what?" he said as he prepared to leave. "I'm a Roman Catholic. I'm going to go straight to my priest and tell him that God's not remote. He's relational."

Now that's what I'm talking about. That man Sid had faith. He believed that God could do something in his life, even though he had no idea what was about to happen to him. Truly, there can be miracles when we believe. The Holy Spirit can give us a mighty revelation of the Father's love in our hearts – one that empowers and compels us to cry out, "Daddy! Oh, my Daddy!"

THE SCIENCE OF HUGGING

It's not just Scripture that teaches us the importance of a dad's hug. Science confirms it too. You may recall that earlier in this book we looked at the new science of fatherhood. I shared how when a child is in their early years they run to Mummy when they want to be comforted, and to Daddy when they want to play.

I also shared that there are chemical rewards in the brain for both parents and children when the mother embraces her child and when the father has rough-and-tumble play. The feel-good and bonding chemicals are released in the brains of all concerned. Some say this is the result of evolutionary processes alone. Others, like me, say this is the way God has also planned things to be.

At this point, some dads may be saying, "Is hugging something that only mothers do?" This is an understandable and legitimate question. If kids are primed to run to Mum when they need a comforting hug, what's the argument, if any, for fathers developing the skill of hugging? I'll tell you. Remember, the science of fatherhood tells us that a father's role is unique. While a mother hugs her child and causes him or her to look inwards, towards her heart if you will, a father hugs his child and encourages him to look outwards, towards the world. A mother's hug has a specific function and purpose: it's the place a child runs to when they feel the need for Mum's soothing and consoling love. A father's hug has an equally specific function and purpose: it's the place a child leaves from and returns to when they explore the big wide world. If a mother's hug is like a hospital, a father's hug is like a harbour. If you've watched the TV reality series on National Geographic, a dad's hug is like Port Protection, Alaska. It's the place from which the locals sail and the haven to which they return.

All this highlights the distinctiveness of a father's hug. Both Mum and Dad have a part to play when it comes to hugs. But when we as dads hug our children, we are effectively turning their faces out towards the adventure that lies beyond us, whether that's a party, pre-school, a first job, or university. We are saying, "I'm always here for you, and you can always come back for a hug. When you do, I'll remind you that I love you before you go out to explore again!"

THE TEENAGE YEARS

All this is especially important when your children get into their teenage years. During this turbulent stage when they need to navigate new and often threatening worlds, it is vital that as dads you are there for them, reassuring them that you love them, reminding them that they are enough. Their foundation of self-esteem is reinforced by you exercising the skill of hugging in the right way at the right time. When you hug them, your teenage children know they are important to you. This reduces three things: (a) the amount of stress hormone called cortisol; (b) the risks of depression; (c) feelings of loneliness. At the same time, it increases (a) resilience; (b) positive self-esteem; (c) good mental health. In fact, we now know that fathers have a much more significant role in this than mothers. Dads need to listen well here: having fun, giving affirmation, investing time, and hugging, these all contribute significantly to a teenager's sense of wellbeing.

This needs to be said over and over because it is so often the case that dads stop hugging their sons and daughters when they approach the teenage years. Recent research has revealed that one in five British dads stop hugging their children once they reach the age of ten. The survey provided some interesting statistics:

- 53% said that they felt their kids were too old for hugs.
- Dads over 55 were less likely to hug their children compared to younger dads (18-34)
- A shift occurs in the way fathers show affection to their children around the time their children become teenagers (14-18), from the physical expression of affection (hugging) to a more verbal one (giving advice and guidance)
- At this age, hugging drops from first to fifth place, behind listening and being attentive to their children and their interests.[20]

This is a trend that needs reversing. Don't stop hugging your child when they approach and enter the teenage years. Yes, you will need to adapt this skill. For example, you'll need to be wise about *where* you exercise it. Teenagers will sometimes be very embarrassed by PDAs from their fathers. You'll need also to be wise about *how*. When their daughters enter puberty, dads shouldn't stop hugging them, but we should hug them in a way that is appropriate because the science tells us they will have a much better chance of avoiding severe stress, depression, and loneliness if we do. They will be able to explore the world from a place of resilience, positive self-esteem, and good mental health. The same is true for sons as well.

So, dads, let's get hugging!

BODY, MIND, AND SPIRIT

I recently saw a news headline that read: "US fentanyl crisis: 'Lack of hugs' behind US opioid overdoses, says Mexico leader." The story here is that there is an epidemic of addiction to fentanyl in the USA, leading to over 70,000 deaths. Fentanyl is a synthetic opioid trafficked by Mexican cartels. The Mexican leader, Andres Manuel Lopez Obrador, has come under intense and increasing pressure from the US government to put a stop to this by designating the drug gangs 'terrorist organisations.' Obrador's response has been to turn the blame back on the USA. His claim is that America has a massive problem with family breakdown. This has led to millions of young people not receiving the love they need and deserve from their parents. If kids were hugged more by their dads, they wouldn't feel the need to make up that deficit by taking a dangerous mood-altering drug. As he put it, "There is a lot of disintegration of families, there is a lot of individualism, there is a lack of love, of brotherhood, of hugs and embraces." His message is that kids take drugs because they haven't been hugged.[21]

As always, the picture is far more complex than these political generalisations and journalistic soundbites would lead you to believe. At the same time, Obrador isn't wrong when he says that a lack of hugs can have serious consequences for a young person's physical, mental, and spiritual health. How does a father's hug help a child in these three areas – body, mind, and spirit?

The **physical** benefits of a father's hug are obvious. When a dad hugs his child, the child feels protected by their father. They feel close to him. They feel reassured. Both the father and the child experience a release of feel-good and bonding chemicals in their brains. This is an obvious physical benefit.

The **mental** and **emotional** benefits of a father's hug are also significant. As we have already seen, a father's hug reduces the chances that a child will feel anxious, stressed, fearful, lonely, and depressed. I sometimes wonder how many therapists would be forced to find another career if fathers hugged their children more.

The **spiritual** benefits of a father's hug are also important, although in a secular society they are least likely to receive attention. What happens to children spiritually when they lose out on a father's demonstrated affection? Remember, trauma isn't just what's done *to* a child. It's also what's not done *for* them. Abuse (what's done *to* them) is unquestionably traumatic. But neglect (what's not done *for* them) can be too. When a child experiences harmful touch (abuse), or the lack of touch altogether (neglect), this can lead to serious problems at a spiritual level. Keep in mind that the spirit is that part of us created to commune with God. If an earthly father hugs a child in a toxic way, or doesn't hug a child at all, this can lead to an understandable rage against the one after whom all fathers derive their name – *the* Father. Father wounds can be devastating at a spiritual level.

No one has proved this case more rigorously or convincingly than the eminent philosopher Paul Vitz. In his ground-breaking book *The Faith of the Fatherless*, he looks at the childhoods of the most famous atheistic philosophers of the twentieth century. Time and again he shows how they suffered paternal deprivation as children. Time and again he shows how they projected the image of their absent or abusive earthly father onto God the Father. His thesis is that ultimately their atheistic and even anti-theistic rage is rooted not so much in philosophy (in cognitive reasoning) but in psychology (in their deep-seated and unresolved wounds from their fathers).[22]

This rings true to me. After over three decades writing and teaching about father wounds and the father heart of God, I have seen time and time again how many people either reject God (and indeed all representations of authority) because they are angry with their father, or they live in a deprived state of communion insofar as they have a relationship with Jesus but not with their Heavenly Father. When dads hug their children in a regular, appropriate, loving way, they build a strong foundation and framework for that child to relate without hindrance to God as their Heavenly Father. When they are physically or emotionally absent, they create the fertile conditions in which the rage against God can grow.

A father's hugs are therefore vital not just for physical and mental health. They are vital for spiritual health too. Regular hugs from a father or a father figure gives lasting BMS (Body, Mind, Spirit) blessings. Maybe Mr Obrador has a point.

DRAWING NEAR TO DAD

If you're a dad and you were deprived of a father's hugs, what can you do to make sure that you don't pass on this tactile deprivation to your own children as they grow up?

In a very real sense, we are returning now to where we began – with Prince Harry's lament. Whether we are convinced by his story or not is not the issue at this point. The fact is Harry has made a vow in his heart, and indeed publicly, that he is going to shower his children with affection because he doesn't want them growing up feeling robbed of a father's love. As far as Harry is concerned, he doesn't want to leave a harmful generational legacy to his children. He is going out of his way to reverse what he sees as a harmful tide.

I had a similar view when I was in my mid-thirties. My adoptive dad was now well advanced with Parkinson's Disease. I was a Vicar in the north of England. One day, I was sitting at my desk preparing a sermon when I was suddenly overcome with a desire to see my father. In the normal course of events, he would have been four or five hours away at home. But it just so happened that he was staying at my cousin's house about 45 minutes away.

I was a young dad at the time with three children, and one on the way. Like Harry, I was determined to ensure they grew up with a dad who hugged them. Like Harry, my father was old-school and Stoical – prone to giving a handshake rather than a full-on hug. But unlike Harry, I decided on a different strategy for dealing with this lack. As I sat at my desk, I felt compelled to go and give Dad a hug and tell him I loved him before it was too late.

So, off I went.

When I arrived, I asked to see Dad on his own. We were given a room with two armchairs in opposite corners. Dad seemed a little confused why I had come to see him.

"Dad," I said. "There's something I need to tell you."

More confusion.

Mixed with concern.

I started to make my way across the floor towards him. If I'm honest, it was the longest and most arduous journey of my life up to that point. Never have I found it harder to move my feet. Dad was not the hugging type. And he was not from the kind of background where "I love you" tripped off the tongue with ease.

"I've come here to tell you that I love you, that I'm grateful to you, and especially that you adopted me."

Dad's eyes glistened.

He seemed to understand.

He somehow got to his feet, shuffled towards me, and threw his arms around my neck.

I held him.

We both cried.

"One thing I will never regret," he said as he pulled away from my grasp and looked into my eyes. "And that's adopting you and Claire." A smile broke out on his stubbled face. "Best decision I ever made," he said, forcing his mouth to form the words.

That moment was healing for both Dad and me. In that embrace, all the sadness about not being hugged in the past disappeared. I gave my dad the gift of my forgiveness. And I offered him a hug in which he hugged me back.

Not long afterwards, Dad died.

Since then, that embrace has become a picture of what true worship is all about. Doesn't the Bible tell us to draw near to God, and he will draw near to us? That's what happens. We take the initiative in worship, making the effort to draw close not to a sick or dying dad but to the Father who is alive forevermore. When we offer him our thanks, our love, he responds by embracing us, holding us in his strong arms of love, those arms that will never let us go.

When we have missed out on a father's embrace in our own childhood, we can draw near to our perfect Heavenly Father. We can find healing for the deficit of demonstrated affection in our own past, ensuring that we don't pass on this lack to future generations.

It's time to experience the great Father's embrace.

He truly hugs the hell out of us.

And he makes us fathers after his own heart.

QUESTION TIME

Look at the four stages of learning:

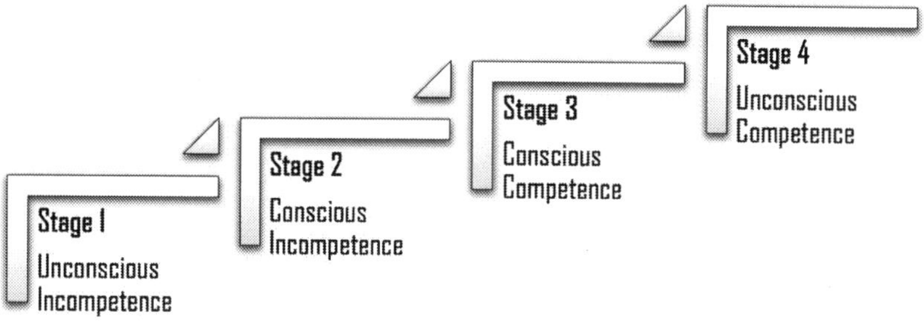

Where are you right now in this specific skill (hugging)?

How are you going to get to the next stage of competence?

What practical changes are you going to make as a dad in the light of what you've just read?

E IS FOR EXAMPLE

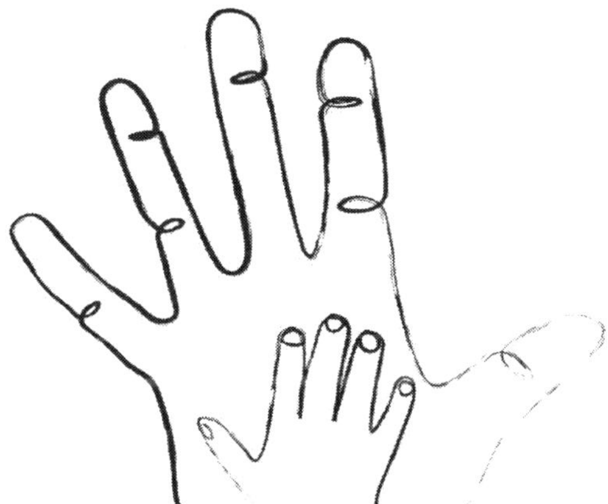

I talk and talk and talk, and I haven't taught people in fifty years what my father taught by example in one week.

Maria Cuomo Cole

6
E IS FOR EXAMPLE

My favourite film when I was a teenager was Stephen Spielberg's *Jaws*. I lost count of how many times I watched it. I've seen it many times since, most recently on my birthday. My wife noticed it was on at the local iMax, so she booked tickets. This was the second time she'd treated me in recent years. In the summer of 2020, when the UK was in full lockdown, a drive-in cinema was set up on the harbour arm in our seaside town. We munched hotdogs while *Jaws* played out in front of the cars, the tell-tale two notes – der-dum – booming through the sound system of our vehicle. Best of all, the outdoor screen was positioned just a few hundred metres away from the raging sea! Our Black Labrador took cover on the back seat as Spielberg's shark chomped its way towards its eventual explosive demise.

I see something new every time I watch *Jaws*, and what struck me most when I watched it again at the local iMax – for the umpteenth time – was a touching scene involving Chief Brody. Brody has just been confronted and slapped by the mother of a boy who was killed by the shark. She is enraged that Brody knew about the threat but failed to close the beaches. Brody had wanted to, but the local mayor had forbidden him, saying that the 4th of July was just around the corner, and closed beaches would mean financial ruin. The town depended on the income from these annual summer holidaymakers.

Brody has therefore been having a very bad day. Now he's sitting at the meal table, his fish supper half eaten, and he's staring into the middle distance. He's dazed by the anger of the grieving mother, shaken by the shark attacks, and confused about how to deal with an aquatic serial killer on the loose around the coast he polices. He has come from the stress-filled streets of the Big Apple to recuperate in a seaside town where the local crime is more about stolen bicycles and bad parking than deadly drugs and assaults. Now he feels as if he's been thrown out of the frying pan into the fire.

Brody is so lost in his thoughts that he fails to notice his little boy. As Mum watches from the door, Brody becomes aware that his young son is studying him. More than that, he is mimicking every movement his dad makes. Brody, realising this, moves his hands, changes his expressions, exaggerates his body language, all the while enjoying the sight of his boy trying to imitate everything he does. It's one of the finest games of copycat between a dad and his child. It ends with Dad saying, "Give us a kiss." Sean replies, "Why?" Dad answers, "Because I need it." Sean obliges, and the scene ends. Brody, whose heart has been cheered, is ready to pursue his quarry once again. If you want to see it, type 'Father and son scene from Jaws' into YouTube.

DADS UNDER DURESS

We have now come to the fifth skill that a dad, or a father figure, needs to learn to cultivate. Just like Sean in the film *Jaws*, children watch their fathers, especially when they are under pressure. Why? Because it is not in seasons of tranquillity but in moments of adversity and extremity that our true character becomes visible. In *Jaws*, Chief Brody was in a situation of intense stress when his youngest son started mimicking him. He was caught between a rock (wanting to close the beaches) and a hard place (needing to keep the local economy alive). He was reeling from the grief-fuelled rage of a bereaved mother. At the meal table, he tried to engage in a calm and rational reflection of his options. His son saw him, studied him, and imitated him.

Another father under great duress was the dad in Luke 15 – the one whose son went to the far country with his inheritance. What's truly exceptional about the father's response is how exemplary it is. In adversity, this father sets a timeless example.

Firstly, he is **patient**. He doesn't lash out at his boy or reprimand him. The boy was scandalously insulting in his behaviour. Asking for your inheritance while your father was still alive was a shameful thing to do. This dad had every right to castigate and chastise him. But he didn't. He exhibited remarkable patience, letting the boy go with his share of the money the two sons would one day inherit. That's extraordinarily patient. What an amazing example!

Secondly, he is **watchful**. This dad spends days and nights looking out for his son, longing for him to return. We are probably to imagine years rather than just months. This dad peered at the shimmering horizon by day, and the moonlit dunes by night. He waited with a broken heart for his son. He didn't reject him or forget him. He pined for him. What an amazing example!

Thirdly, he is **compassionate**. When he at last sees what he has been hoping for – the silhouette of his son – he does not lose his temper. He feels empathy. This emotion leads to motion. It causes him to run towards his son. Why does he run? Because the villagers, if they get to him first, will treat him harshly. This dad wants to prevent this, so he lifts his robe and runs. What an amazing example!

Fourthly, he is **affectionate**. This dad doesn't subject his boy to a volley of verbal reprimands. He throws his arms around his son and kisses him. This is again quite remarkable. The dad had every right to lecture his child on the consequences of his reckless rebellion. But he doesn't. He holds him tightly. He hugs the hell out of him instead. What an amazing example this father sets!

Finally, he is **forgiving**. When he tells his servants to fetch the V.I.P. robe, he tells them to give it to him. As soon as this robe is covering the boy's shame, it says to all those watching that the dad forgives his son totally, instantly, unconditionally. Instead of meting out judgment, this father acts mercifully. That this is radical love is an understatement. What an amazing example!

Why does Jesus portray the father acting in this way?

For two reasons.

He wants dads to understand the importance of setting a great example for their children. When they are under duress, dads should not fly off the handle. They should be patient, watchful, compassionate, affectionate, and forgiving.

And they should do this because this dad isn't just an example for all other dads to follow. He's also a representation of God the Father. Our Heavenly Father is patient, watchful, compassionate, affectionate, and forgiving with all of us. He is what Jesus called "the perfect Father." He sets the finest example of all.

SHOULDERS VERSUS SERMONS

Sometimes we are tempted as dads to believe that it is through what we say that we set the best example for our children. We want them to develop a strong moral compass, especially in this mad and chaotic world where the moral frameworks of the past have been rejected in favour of a wholly subjective view of right and wrong. As dads, we know that the old moral certainties have been consigned by society to the trash heap. We know that our kids are going to be sorely tempted and severely tested. In such a complex and compromising landscape, it is too easy to try and compensate by over-moralizing. When our kids mess up, we are inclined to lecture rather than love them.

But this is exactly what the dad in Luke 15 does *not* do. He never moralizes when his son comes home. He doesn't remind his boy that he has sinned badly by wasting his dad's hard-earned wealth on hedonistic, excessive, and addictive behaviours. He does not preach a trenchant message about the dangers of drink or the seductive and destructive perils of prostitution. No, instead of a sermon, he provides a shoulder. He chooses affection over correction.

This reminds me of a conversation I once had in Northern Ireland. I was preaching at a celebration at a large Pentecostal church in Belfast. The other speaker was Ruth Graham, one of the daughters of the late, great Billy Graham – the finest Christian evangelist of the twentieth century. After I had given a talk about Luke 15, Ruth told me a story. She had messed up very badly in her life. She was into her second divorce and her life was in tatters. At her lowest, she decided to go home and see her father. She was terrified as she pulled up in her car at the front of the house. As it turned out, she needn't have been. Billy Graham came out the door and ran to her. He held her tightly and welcomed her home. Ruth was overwhelmed by his example.[23]

I have never forgotten that story. Ruth told it again at her father's funeral a few years ago. She tells it in her wonderful book about being less judgmental and more compassionate to the many wounded and messed up people around us. It's called *In Every Pew there's a Broken Heart*. So often preachers can be self-righteous and condescending rather than vulnerable and authentic. Dads catch this soul-destroying virus and act in the same way with their children. Instead of empathy, we demonstrate morality. Instead of a shoulder, we give a sermon. Never forget the dad in Luke 15, or Billy Graham for that matter. When it comes to setting an example, actions speak louder than words, especially when our kids make mistakes.

LEARNING FROM FAILURE

Let's be realistic. Our children are going to make mistakes. They are going to fall, and they are going to fail. I'm afraid this is life in the real world. No amount of giving them everything they want, or trying to remove every obstacle to success, will inoculate them against failure. They are going to stumble. What you should not do is make them feel worse than they already do when they come to you for help. The example you set in these critical moments of stressful adversity will be something they study. Don't make them feel like abject sinners and failures. Show them how they can learn from their mistakes. Show them how they can harness failure in a positive way. In short, show them how to turn a mess into a message, as Ruth Graham has done.

In the first chapter, I mentioned one of my favourite nonfiction authors – Matthew Syed. Matthew wrote a book called *Black Box Thinking*. If you remember, he uses plane crashes as a picture of dealing with failure. When you mess up, study the black boxes, learn from the mistakes, and make sure you roll out the lessons in all areas of your life. That's "black box thinking."

Matthew has not only written titles like these, geared to adult readers, he has also been writing ones that communicate to younger readers, especially those in the middle grade age group (8-12). One of these is entitled *You are Awesome*, subtitled, 'Find your Confidence and Dare to be Brilliant at Almost Anything.'

Just the other day, I was looking at Twitter when I saw something quite wonderful. A father had been listening to a podcast in which Matthew Syed was being interviewed. As a result, he had bought a copy of *You are Awesome* for his eleven-year-old son. He then wrote in a Twitter post that he had been "absolutely blown away" when he found a handwritten note by his bed. It was from his boy.

"Thank you, daddy.

To daddy, thank you for getting me the book because it has told me that mistakes are just another way of doing things.

It has also told me that having a fixed mindset doesn't leave room for the positives in life.

Thank you so much."

The father added that this was from a boy who's struggled to reconcile failure and isn't a big book reader.

Matthew Syed simply wrote, "Made my day. Thanks."

What a wonderful story. Our role as dads is to be real and vulnerable. Our role is to create an atmosphere in which our kids can do some black box thinking. Our role is to turn them from victims into victors, to give them not a sermon but a shoulder.

BE REAL, NOT RELIGIOUS

If I'm honest, this is something I didn't fully understand when my children were navigating their teenage years. I was a Vicar at the time. I spent much of my life preaching. So, guess what they got from me when they messed up? A sermon, not a shoulder.

One of my children became extremely rebellious during these years. In fact, things got so bad that I was summoned to the local school – a school where I spoke regularly at the morning assemblies. The child concerned – whom we will call X, to protect their dignity and honour – had messed up so badly, the headteacher was given no other option. She was going to have to ask them to leave.

I remember sitting in the headteacher's office while she shared what X had done. There was no going back. X had gone too far. What had confused the headteacher was why.

"It's strange," she said. "Normally, children only behave like X when they come from broken or dysfunctional homes. But that's not the case here. I've been confused by that."

She paused to look at me. There was genuine compassion in her eyes. Then she said, "Until I spoke with one of my deputies, who is the daughter of an Anglican bishop."

I raised my eyebrows.

"She told me that there's another category besides children

from broken and dysfunctional homes."

"What's that?" I asked.

"Preacher's kids. They can go off the rails because it's just too hard to follow their parent's religious beliefs when few of the friends in their peer group subscribe to them."

As she said that, I knew it was true. I had brought my kids up in a religious home. Our house (the vicarage) was on the same carpark as the church building. For my kids, there was therefore no escape from it all. It was only when years later I messed up and failed, the religious mask came off and I started being real with them. Last summer, one of them said, "Dad, it's so good getting to know the real you." They were mid-thirties when they said that.

One of the biggest mistakes I made as a father during those years was being religious instead of real. I set a poor example in that regard. Instead of being vulnerable and empathetic, I came across as pious and self-righteous. If you're in a similar situation, my advice to you is, *be real*. The dad who appears perfect all the time sets unattainable standards, and in the process becomes unreachable. The dad who has strong beliefs but who at the same time isn't afraid of being vulnerable and authentic, that dad is much more accessible.

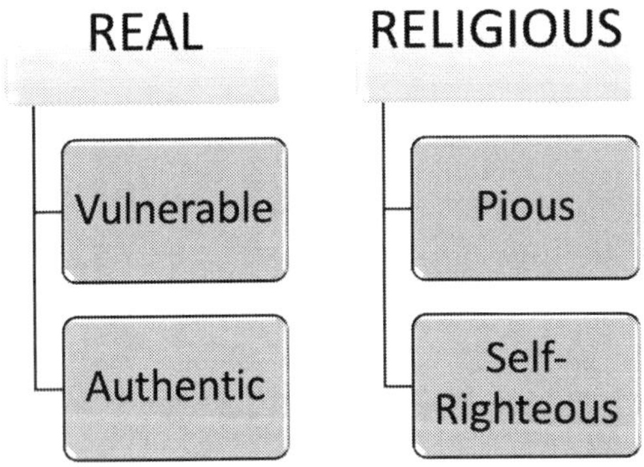

Being real means being empathetic and listening to our children when they are trying to be loyal to what you're teaching them while at the same time being accepted by their friends. This is an unbelievably complicated terrain. Nothing is to be gained by moralizing. When they mess up – as they surely will – be there for them. Be honest. Tell them your own stories of failure. But show them also that it's not falling that ruins us; it's failing to get up and go again.

If you want to set a great example, give them a shoulder, not a sermon. Demonstrate the law of love not the love of law in the way you father your children. Don't be a *Pharisee*.

UP, OUT, AND IN

When it comes to setting an example, what should dads prioritise? The answer is love. But love is a very wishy-washy word these days. It's used to justify almost any and every dysfunction. So, let me be clear about what I mean. Love means giving true and positive worth to someone or something. Where, then, should this kind of love be directed? The answer is provided by Jesus in his famous answer to a question put to him by a religious man. He asked, "What's the greatest of all God's commandments?" Jesus's answer in Mark 12:29-31 is, like everything else he ever said, very revealing. He told him, *"The most important commandment is this: 'Listen, O Israel! The LORD our God is the one and only LORD. And you must love the LORD your God with all your heart, all your soul, all your mind, and all your strength.' The second is equally important: 'Love your neighbour as yourself.' No other commandment is greater than these."*

When it comes to the objects of our love, we should note that Jesus commands us firstly to love God, secondly to love others, and thirdly to love ourselves. A dad needs to learn over time to set a good and healthy example in all three of these areas. I call these the UP (God), OUT (others) and IN (ourselves) dimensions.

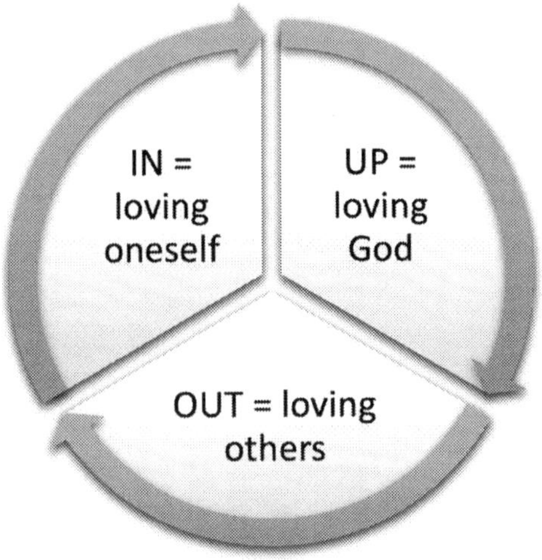

Thinking now of my adoptive dad, I can safely say he set me a good example in all three of these.

Firstly, he set an example to me of loving God. He had not been a Christian as a younger man, but when he fought in the Far East in World War 2, a Gurkha rifleman – a Christian called Moto – laid down his life for my dad. This made a deep and lasting impression of him. When Dad returned to Oxford University after the war, and took up his studies of English Literature again, C.S. Lewis befriended him. Lewis was Britain's most famous Christian at the time, and it wasn't long before Dad became a committed Christian. He set a fine example for all of us in that regard. I went on to become a Vicar. My twin sister is a committed Christian. My older brother is the assistant warden of his local church. Clearly, something of his faith rubbed off on us!

Secondly, he set an example to me of loving others. He married Mum after the war when both were in their mid-thirties. When I became a teenager, Mum went through years of clinical depression, including suicidal thoughts. Dad stayed with her and supported her all the way, even though Mum's behaviour could be very challenging. He truly loved others, starting with his own family. As a headteacher, he loved the children and the staff, and was greatly loved and fondly remembered in turn, especially for his great kindness at school. He set a fine example to me when it came to loving others.

Thirdly, he set an example to me of loving himself. If love means giving true and positive worth to someone or something, he certainly did that in relation to God, and to others (especially his wife), but he also did in relation to himself. He did not hate himself. He did not regard himself as worthless. He had a measured, healthy, positive sense of self-worth. He knew he was loved by his Heavenly Father, just as he had been by his earthly dad. Dad set a great example.

A HEALTHY REALISM

If you were fortunate enough to have a good dad, don't be starry eyed. It's important that you don't idealise your father. He has or had flaws too. You and I need to be realistic about these defects if we aren't to replicate his negative traits and pass on generational patterns of unhelpful or even toxic behaviour.

Was my dad a bad example in any way? The answer is inevitably yes. If there is one area that I would single out - doing so in a spirit of honouring my father (as the Scriptures command) - it's this. He was not emotionally intelligent at times. There were moments in my childhood when Mum was beginning to feel the first hints of a terrible depression. The tell-tale sign of this was a volcanic rage. Mum would start shouting and screaming. The trigger would usually be some tiny and even trivial incident which stirred up a deeply held belief in her lack of worth. It could be anything, from one of us children not setting the table in exactly the right way, to one of us unwittingly making her feel left out. She had been badly treated as a child – made to feel of little intelligence and value in comparison to her brothers. This sense of isolation and devaluation made her feel a profound sense of shame. She believed the lie that she wasn't worthy of love and belonging. Much of this came from her Victorian father who, by his behaviour, made Mum come to feel that she should neither be seen nor heard.

When this trauma was triggered, Mum would fly into an uncontrollable rage. What did Dad do? The answer, I'm afraid, is nothing. What Mum needed at these moments was for him to hold her and reassure her that she was not alone, that she was heard and loved. But he didn't. He was physically present but emotionally absent. He simply didn't react at all. Why? Because he was dealing with his own stuff, and that stuff was traumatic too.

It took me a long time before I realised why Dad reacted as he did. When he became a POW (Prisoner of War), he suffered terribly for a period of nearly three years. That he survived was not just testament to his resilience. It was also a mark of his adaptability. He came to realise very quickly that the best way to avoid beatings, incarceration, torture, and execution was to look away when one of the enemy officers was enraged by something. Look away, look down, look anywhere but at the person kicking off about this or that. He would disengage. Not say a word. Disassociate we would call it today.

And that's what Dad did after the war when we were kids and Mum was shouting. Dad reactivated his survival strategy. He removed his emotion chip. The problem with that is he set a bad example. During my first marriage, my ex-wife's biggest complaint was that I would not react emotionally when there were situations of stress in her life. I would be disengaged. In this respect, I was simply re-enacting my father's lack of emotional intelligence. His unawareness about what he was doing (or better still, not doing) and why became mine. A bad example became an unhelpful pattern until I realised what I was doing.

WHAT SCIENCE TELLS US

This points to one of the unique roles that a father has in relation to the skill of setting a good example. What science now tells us is this, that the way our dads relate to our mums can create the foundations in a boy's mind, and a girl's mind too, for their expectations and experiences in adult life. Boys look at their fathers. They learn how to treat girls from the way their father treats their mother. If Dad looks down on Mum and treats her as a lesser being, we shouldn't be surprised to find sons growing up with misogynistic beliefs and behaviours. If Dad treats Mum with honour and respect, we shouldn't be surprised to find sons growing up with healthy beliefs about women.

A not dissimilar dynamic plays out in relation to daughters. Daughters also watch the way Dad treats Mum. Over time, they see from both his attitudes and actions how men are supposed to treat women. If Dad mistreats Mum, his daughter will start to believe the very dangerous lie that this is how things are meant to be. Having become the normal in her childhood, she will often look to make it the normal in her adult relationships. But if Dad loves, honours, respects Mum, that will be her normal in childhood, and she will subconsciously look to recreate that same narrative in her adult relationships too.

We should note two other things. Firstly, the way a father relates to his child establishes patterns of connecting and disconnecting. If a dad employs what's called 'the still face' – looking away from his infant child, emotionally detached – don't be surprised if that child grows up and employs the same traits in their adult romantic relationships. This is something that two brilliant scientists - Sue Johnson and Ed Tronick - have confirmed. Go to YouTube and find "Love Sense: from Infant to Adult." Watch how a man employs "still face" tactics with his wife when she is upset. She wants him to engage, but his face is quite literally still, and turned away from her. This is a pattern established by a parent in his childhood. As Sue Johnson says, "science tells us clearly that bonding goes from the cradle to the grave."

Secondly, science also tells us that when a father invests in an emotionally healthy way with his teenage daughter it has a big impact on whether she chooses to behave promiscuously. A study at the University of Arizona has found that quality time with fathers reduces the incidences of "risky sexual behaviours" in their daughters. Risky sexual behaviour includes the following: having sex without a condom, having sex while intoxicated, having multiple sexual partners, and becoming pregnant before age 19.

The lead author of this peer-reviewed study, Bruce Ellis, has come up with some startling conclusions about invested dads and their teenage daughters. He says, "When it comes to girls and their decisions about sex, it turns out a father's influence really does matter." Dads who are physically present and emotionally engaged help their daughters to act wisely and responsibly. Conversely, daughters who lack a dad like this also lack the brakes and bulwarks that prevent them from rushing headlong into promiscuity. As Ellis says, "Girls who receive lower quality fathering tend to engage in more risky sexual behaviour in adolescence." Once again, then, we see science confirming that a father's example is of critical importance in their child's development. Learning the example skill is a prerequisite for fathers.[24]

BACK TO SPIELBERG

We began this chapter with the scene in *Jaws* where Chief Brody realizes that his youngest son Sean is mimicking his every move. It is a moment of tenderness between brutal attacks by the Great White Shark off the Amity coast. It is also a lasting reminder of how important it is for us dads to realise that our children watch us, observing how we respond to situations, especially those involving more than a fair degree of stress. How we react becomes a template for them, just as how we relate to them, and indeed their mother, becomes a blueprint for their adult romantic relationships.

People are often hard on Spielberg when it comes to the theme of fatherhood. The standard narrative is this: that he had a poor experience of being fathered (which he did) and that he allows this to come out in many of his films. It is true that his dad was emotionally disengaged from him when he was young, and it is also true that he didn't show any appreciation or approval for his son until his fellow workers caused him to see what his son had achieved.

Another thing that's true is that some of Spielberg's films portray fractured relationships between children and their distracted and disengaged dads. In *Close Encounters of the Third Kind*, the father becomes obsessed with extra-terrestrial beings and vessels, to the detriment of his relationship with his wife and children. In *Indiana Jones and the Last Crusade*, the entire film is about Indie's relationship with his father (Sean Connery) – an emotionally and often physically absent figure throughout Indie's life.

It is perhaps inevitable that Spielberg's experience of being poorly fathered has impacted his films. When his parent's marriage fell apart, he was traumatized by the sound of their arguments. Fifteen years of complete estrangement from his dad followed. It shouldn't therefore surprise us that in films like *Catch Me if You Can* the theme of the absent father plays such a critical role. But what's not true is the suggestion that this is the only way Spielberg portrays fathers. Even as early as *Jaws*, we see Brody being a protective, devoted, present, and affectionate dad. There isn't therefore just regret in his films (the fathers who are not there). There is longing (fathers who *are* there). While *E.T.* expresses the former, *Hook* (as we saw earlier in this book) expresses the latter. Indeed, in *Hook*, the father resolves to become invested in the skills of fun and time. There is redemption.

Interestingly, this has been true of Spielberg himself. When he became a father, he found himself mimicking his own father's behaviour. He was absent a lot, and when he was around, he was moralizing and lecturing his children, preaching there's only one way, as his own father had. He went with his wife to therapy and, with the help of his psychologist, broke away from his 1940s template of caregiving to a much more enlightened approach to fatherhood. "I began becoming like my father," he said, but then he broke the mould.[25]

CAPTAIN JOHN MILLER

Perhaps this is why Spielberg's later films are more balanced not just in their portrayal of dads, but also of father figures. By father figures I mean those people who are not the biological father of those younger souls they care for, but stand-in dads. There are so many of these in the world today, it's only fair and right to celebrate the stepfathers, adoptive fathers, foster fathers, and substitute dads too.

Here I come into land with one of the greatest of all WW2 films, *Saving Private Ryan*. What is Captain John Miller if he is not a father figure to the band of brothers he leads? Miller is played by Tom Hanks, who has become a kind of Hollywood father figure in his own right. But in Spielberg's classic, he is a father figure not just to his men, but most of all to Private Ryan himself, played by Matt Damon. Miller searches for Ryan as a father would his lost child. When he finds him, he protects him as if he was his own too. And in the end, when Miller gives his life for Ryan, Miller tells Ryan to "earn this." In other words, don't let this self-sacrifice be wasted. Live a good life. Put others first. Follow my example. Do to others what I have done for you."

What we've been looking at in this chapter is the importance of setting a healthy example. This can be done by both fathers and father figures. Ultimately, the greatest example is set when we love others. When dads put others before themselves – especially their children, or those in the position of a child – he transmits something powerful to the human soul. Love is the key here.

Not the sentimental and often selfish iteration of love we see so often today. But self-forgetful love. Show your child, or the person you're caring for, their true and positive worth. Show love in the UP, OUT, IN dimensions of life. Show the next generation the truth of what Jesus said, that "greater love has no man than this, that he lay down his life for his friends."

That's the kind of love we need to see today.

As the late great Burt Bacharach sang, "What the world needs now is love, sweet love."

As a dad or father figure, make that your song.

QUESTION TIME

Look at the four stages of learning:

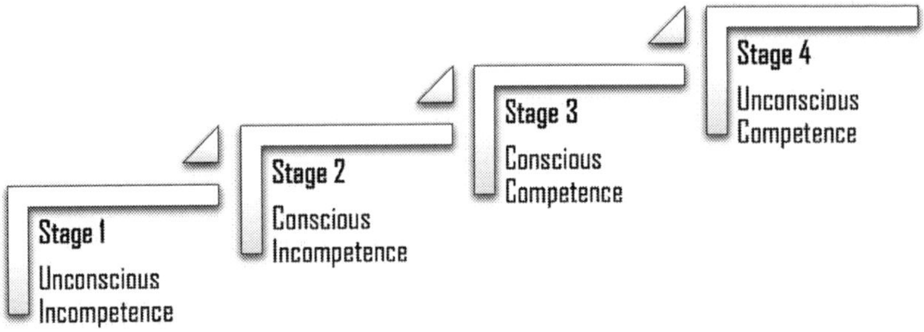

Where are you right now in this specific skill (setting an example)?

How are you going to get to the next stage of competence?

What practical changes are you going to make as a dad in the light of what you've just read?

R IS FOR RULES

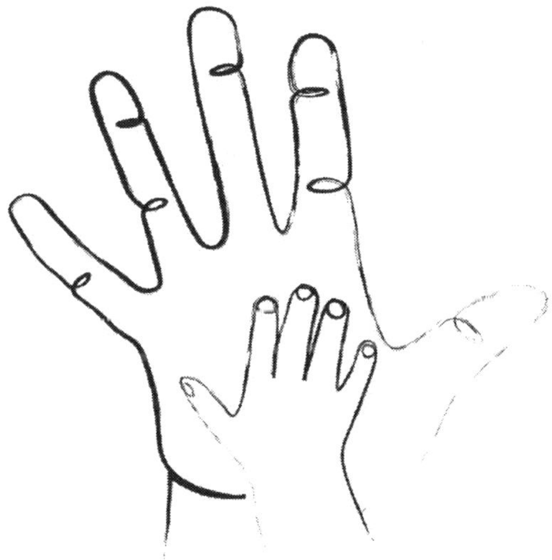

Who ever heard of a child who is never
disciplined by its father?

Hebrews 12:7

7
R IS FOR RULES

Something strange was going on with the young bull elephants in a park in South Africa. Concerned about the growing numbers of elephants generally, officials had decided to leave the larger bull elephants at the Kruger National Park and relocate many of the females and all the young bull elephants in Pilanesburg National Park. This solved one problem – thinning the ranks – but it also created another. The young bull elephants in the new location started to behave in a wild and destructive manner. Park rangers found the dead bodies of white rhinos. They suspected poachers at first, but then it became clear that it was the young male elephants. Having set up cameras, they discovered that groups of delinquent juvenile elephants were going on the rampage, chasing the rhinos, gauging them with their tusks, and stomping them to death. Such behaviour is very rare.

The rangers and park officials met together to discuss why this was happening at Pilanesburg. They concluded that the most likely reason was that they had relocated the juveniles but had neglected to place any older bull elephants with them.

The rangers went back to Kruger National Park and transported some of the older bull elephants to Pilanesburg National Park. The delinquent and violent actions of the young male elephants stopped immediately. The older males showed the young males that killing rhinos was not what elephants do. They modelled a more peaceful and self-controlled way of behaving. As the juveniles followed their older, dominant role models around the park, they reverted to true elephant-like behaviour.

Some years later in New York, people noticed that groups of young men were behaving in an aggressive and anti-social manner in Central Park. They were operating with a kind of herd instinct, committing crimes and generally being a nuisance. A man called Dr Horn remembered what had happened to the young bull elephants in the South African parks. In an article entitled 'Of Elephants and Men,' he asked the following question: "Where have all the fathers gone?" He concluded that the reason why these young men were harassing and victimizing others – especially women – was because they had no older male role models in their lives to restrain their aggression and to teach them what is and isn't human behaviour. Most of these juvenile male delinquents were, in short, fatherless.[26]

This is entirely in line with my own experience. Visiting male prisons in both the UK and the USA, I have found that somewhere in the region of 85% of the inmates have lacked any positive experience of being fathered. On one occasion, I was speaking to a room full of young men in a prison chapel outside Bristol, UK. I asked how many of them had a dad. Only one raised their hand.

Another time, a friend of mine involved in a prison chaplaincy team in another part of the UK decided to offer every inmate a card for Mother's Day. If the inmate wrote a message of thanks to Mum and put the address on the envelope provided, the chaplaincy team would put a stamp on the envelope and post it to their mothers. When the team asked how many of the young men in the prison wanted to accept the offer, every one of them said yes.

The team decided they would offer the same thing to the young men for Father's Day. They sent out a form to every inmate asking if they wanted to have a card and an envelope to fill. It was, they said, an opportunity to say thank you to Dad for all he had done. The response? Not one prisoner said they wanted a card.

Today, we have a serious problem with young people being unruly, aggressive, anti-social, and violent. One of the reasons why this is happening is because the fathers who could offer an example to them are absent. What would happen if dads were empathetically present and offered their children love-based boundaries?

DADS AND BOUNDARIES

As dads, we often shy away from developing the skill of rule and boundary setting, but we should remember that God's fatherhood, after which our own is derived, is not just characterised by loving affection. It's also characterised by loving authority. You can't have one without the other when it comes to fathering. A healthy father gives their children boundaries as well as hugs. If you're a father figure in a sports context, it's no good comforting your younger proteges when they get injured but telling them to ignore the boundary markers on the field. You need to coach them to respect the referee, not just to enjoy the rewards. You need to embrace loving authority not just loving affection. If you don't do this, you will have mayhem.

God's fathering involves both authority *and* affection. It's both a matter of setting rules as well as expressing compassion. Look at God's relationship with the people of Israel. On the one hand, he decrees that he wants to adopt them out of all the nations of the earth, all because he has set his affection upon them (Deuteronomy 7:7-8). At the same time, he tells them that there are family rules. These rules are not intended to punish or oppress them. They are designed to help them succeed in life. Put another way, these rules are not for their punishment but for their protection. So, the ten rules that God expects his adopted children to observe are love-based not law-based requirements. They are designed to keep us within the boundaries where true blessing can be found at every level of life:

- You shall have no other gods before me.
- You shall not make for yourself an image in the form of anything in heaven above or on the earth beneath or in the waters below.
- You shall not misuse the name of the LORD your God, for the LORD will not hold anyone guiltless who misuses his name.
- Remember the Sabbath day by keeping it holy. Six days you shall labour and do all your work, but the seventh day is a sabbath to the LORD your God.
- Honour your father and your mother, so that you may live long in the land the LORD your God is giving you.
- You shall not murder.
- You shall not commit adultery.
- You shall not steal.
- You shall not give false testimony against your neighbour.
- You shall not covet your neighbour's house. You shall not covet your neighbour's wife, or his male or female servant, his ox or donkey, or anything that belongs to your neighbour.

AUTHORITY AND AFFECTION

As earthly fathers we are called to imitate our Heavenly Father. In other words, we are called not only to demonstrate loving affection. We are also called to embody loving authority. If you have affection without authority, you will bring up children who think that they can do anything they want without facing the consequences for their poor choices. If you have authority without affection, you will raise sons and daughters who end up wounded and resentful, all because you drifted from being a person who exercises loving authority and became authoritarian instead. The effective and competent father displays both loving affection and loving authority. He is a both-and person.

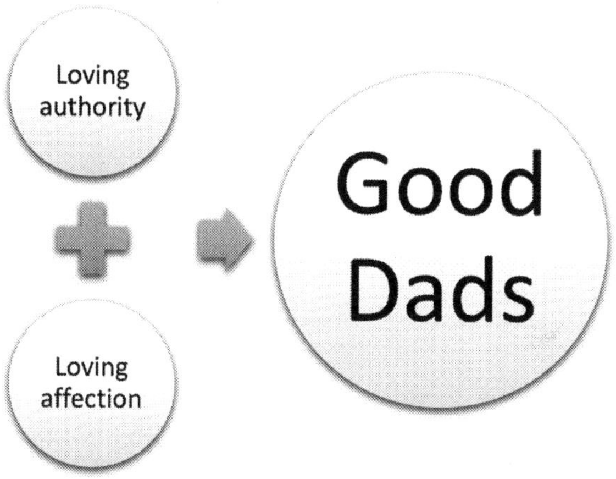

One of the best examples of this combination is the father in the Book of Proverbs. This book forms part of what's known as the Wisdom Literature of the Old Testament. Much of it consists of the wise advice given by a father (perhaps a "spiritual father") to his children. It begins in Proverbs 1:8 with, "My child, listen when your father corrects you." What follows is a father's combination of loving affection and loving authority, and it covers varied subjects.

In Proverbs 1:10, the father sets some healthy rules about keeping away from toxic peers.

My child, if sinners entice you,
turn your back on them!

In Proverbs 2:2-3, the father sets some healthy rules about

making wisdom a priority in life.

My child, listen to what I say,
and treasure my commands.

In Proverbs 3:11-12, the father encourages his child to accept God's fatherly correction when they transgress.

My child, don't reject the LORD's discipline,
and don't be upset when he corrects you.
For the LORD corrects those he loves,
just as a father corrects a child in whom he delights.

In Proverbs 5:7-8, 15, this same father sets some boundaries for his sons when it comes to sexual promiscuity.

So now, my sons, listen to me.
Never stray from what I am about to say:
Stay away from her!
Don't go near the door of her house!
Drink water from your own well -
share your love only with your wife.

In Proverbs 10:4-5, this same father sets healthy life rules about being hard-working rather than lazy.

Lazy people are soon poor;
hard workers get rich.
A wise youth harvests in the summer,
but one who sleeps during harvest is a disgrace.

All these are a combination of authority and affection.

GROWING IN WISDOM

All this sounds very easy, doesn't it? But what happens if your child turns out to be unconventional, complex, untypical? What if they aren't conformists? What if they buck the trends and break the moulds? What if they're different from what you're used to, and different from what you expected them to become? What if they're neurodivergent? What if they're not happy in their bodies? What if they struggle with profound mental health issues and suicidal ideation? What if they are not the kind of child that fits into mainstream schools?

There are three words that often crop up in the Book of Proverbs: wisdom, understanding, and discernment. The father in the book encourages his children to grow in each of these. But the truth is this: if a person is to become a good and healthy father, they must cultivate each of these too. As soon as fathers think they know everything, they're in trouble. Some children require much more wisdom than others. If you believe in simple black-and-white categories, you'll almost certainly fall at the first hurdle. If, however, you're prepared to grow in wisdom, you will succeed in life and so will your child.

Let's take a famous example. One of my favourite novels of the twentieth century is Harper Lee's story, *To Kill a Mockingbird*. It is a tale primarily about a lawyer trying to defend an African American man in a culture where racism is rampant and where justice is rare for people of colour. It is also a film about fatherhood. The lawyer, Atticus Finch, is a dad to two children. One of them, his daughter Scout, is far from typical. Growing up without a mother, she lacks a feminine role model in the home and has become something of a rebellious tomboy. In fact, for Atticus, fathering his daughter has become as complex and challenging as defending his client. It has caused him to lean on wisdom at his own house as well as in the courthouse.

The 1962 film version of this classic novel stars Gregory Peck as Atticus and Mary Badham as Scout. One of my favourite scenes takes place as Scout is preparing to go to school. She runs out onto the deck and bursts into tears. Her father comes out to her. She tells him that she's not going back to that school anymore. Atticus consoles her. Yesterday was just the first day. It'll get better.

"I don't care," she cries. "Everything went wrong."

Scout recites a list of grievances, including the fact that the teacher told her that her dad was teaching her to read the wrong way. That really gets to Scout. She loves these times with her dad.

Atticus puts his arm around her shoulder.

Scout continues her lament, "If I go to school, you'll never be able to read to me."

"You know what a compromise is?" Atticus asks.

"Bending the law?"

Atticus smiles and says no. "It's an agreement reached by mutual consent. Here's the way it works. You concede the necessity of going to school and *we'll* keep right on reading the same every night, just as we always have. Is that a bargain?"

Scout looks at her dad. They nod and smile. The narrator – the grownup Scout – concludes, "There just didn't seem to be anything or anyone that Atticus couldn't explain."

That's *wisdom!*

Atticus leaned on wisdom gleaned as a lawyer (the idea of a legal compromise) and set some love-based rules. He was a legal man, so his rules could have been law-based. But wisdom means exercising authority in a loving not a legalistic way, so he chose love. Atticus is a great example of a father who grows in wisdom - a father who exercises loving authority as well as loving affection.[27]

GROWING IN UNDERSTANDING

I have known David and Carrie Grant ever since I spoke at their church in London nearly two decades ago. David and Carrie are famous musicians, singers, and voice coaches in the UK. They have appeared regularly as judges on TV, and they run a weekly radio programme. They are both committed Christians. They are also the proud parents of four children – three birth children, one adopted. Three of their children are neurodiverse. Two are also transgender. To say that their lives as parents has involved immense challenges would be an understatement. They have learned to live in the grey areas of life where there's mystery and ambiguity. The old black-and-white thinking used by parents of neurotypical children hasn't worked on the coalface of such complexities. They have had to discard their traditional expectations of what a family looks like and start all over again.

Put simply, David and Carrie have had to grow in *understanding*. As they've watched some of their children feel excluded at school, depressed and even suicidal, unhappy with the sex assigned to them at birth, wrestling with profound issues of identity, they have had to adapt. This has involved a humble and costly process of growing in understanding as they've sought help from counsellors, support groups, and experts in the relevant fields. The fact that they have not tried to impose more conventional rules and boundaries on their children has been instrumental in navigating these turbulent years. They have learned to pray, "change *us*", rather than "change *them*." That stark humility has given them the grace to listen empathetically to their children as well as attentively to those who know more about these contemporary complexities. This has led them to morph as parents. They are now releasing a highly publicised book on their newfound understanding called *A Very Modern Family*.

David and Carrie describe themselves as "Warrior Parents." This does not mean what some of you may think it means. It does not mean that they are conservative vigilantes. It means that they have had had to fight for their children's rights to be who and what they have been created to be. It means that they have had to fight for their children to get places in schools best suited to their unique profiles. It means they have had to fight for their parenting values in the face of confusion and consternation even from some of their own family members. It means they have had to fight for their kids in the face of the criticisms of those whose religious operating system is more inflexible. David Grant is a Warrior Dad in that sense, and Carrie is a Warrior Mum. And in this, they are utterly commendable.

David and Carrie have therefore grown in understanding. This understanding, much of which has involved listening to their children and learning from them, has shaped the way they exercise the skill of rule setting. Their rules may look different from yours, but they are equally valid, not least because they have been forged on the anvil of adversity and in the face of life-and-death issues. In many ways, their success as parents derives from the fact that they have refused to see their children as problems to fix, but as people to help. As they put it, "Truly hearing our children is a skill we continually strive to master. By nature, we are problem-solvers, practical, hands on, "we've got the answer to this" kind of people. This can be really helpful but can also be a real hinderance to our children. We have had to learn to sit alongside them in their thoughts and feelings."[28]

David and Carrie Grant are a great example of parents who have grown in understanding. This understanding has shaped their fusion of loving authority and loving affection. It has informed the way they have set and maintained rules and boundaries too.

GROWING IN DISCERNMENT

By now, you may be wondering when we are going to return to the parable of the devoted father in Luke 15, especially since it's the foundation of this entire book! Well, you don't have to wait any longer. We're heading there now.

The father in Luke 15 has, without doubt, exercised loving authority and loving affection in the way he has brought up his two sons. We can tell he has shown them affection by the way he responds to the younger son when he comes home, and the older son when he complains about the party his father has thrown. We can also tell that he has exercised loving authority as well. This is a Jewish household, after all, and one of the ten commandments has required both boys to honour their father. When the younger son comes to his dad and asks for his share of the inheritance, this involves him breaking the rules. Not only has he broken one of the ten commandments by dishonouring his dad, he has also broken a cultural rule. In those days, asking a father for your share of the inheritance *while he was still alive* was an utterly shameful thing to do. It was the same as saying, "I wish you were dead." The boy's failure to wait until his father had passed was scandalous. His request was the same as saying, "Drop dead, dad!"

Given that this is a drastic and brutal crossing of moral boundaries and a cruel fracturing of cultural rules, why is it that the father doesn't ground him? Why does he not simply say no? Why does he not withdraw all privileges for his son? Why does he not castigate him for shaming him in such a harsh and thankless way?

The answer, I propose, has everything to do with *discernment*. You see, when flagrant acts of rebellion like this occur, a father needs to discern what lies behind them. In this, and indeed every other case, there are essentially two possible roots.

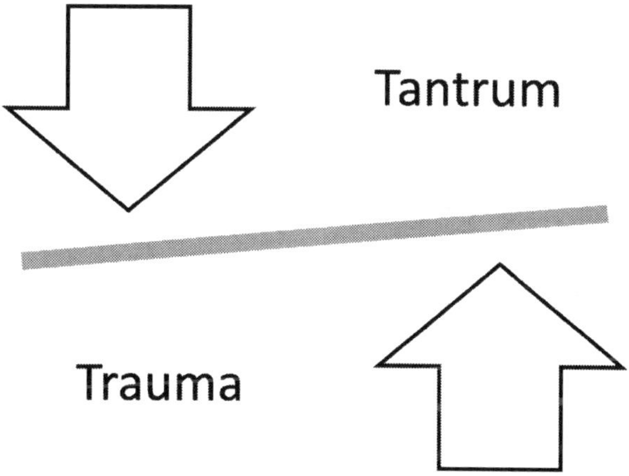

The first root of the boy's rebellion could have been a tantrum. We are all fundamentally selfish people, or what the Bible calls sinners. This is something genetically inherited. The most obvious indication of this is the behaviour of a child when their language skills begin to develop. What are some of the first words children say?

"No!"

"Mine!"

"I want....!"

The father, listening to his son's request, could have discerned that the root cause was his son's inherent and inherited sinfulness. If that had been the case, the boy would certainly have been denied his request and disciplined in an appropriate way.

What, then, is the second root? It's trauma. Sometimes a child will rebel against love because of a traumatic wound. What kind of trauma might have been behind this son's breaking of the rules?

I wonder if you've ever noticed something strange about this parable – namely, the absence of the mother. The *mama* is a potent presence in every Jewish household – the glue that keeps the family together. She imparts more to her child than a hundred teachers ever could. Where is this mother figure? It's a good question. Her absence is very noticeable. Her silence is deafening.

TRAUMA AND DISSENT

One of Rembrandt's most famous paintings depicts the return of the prodigal son. It is a masterpiece for so many reasons. As numerous scholars have pointed out, the father's hands are very carefully painted. As the father drapes his arms over the boys shoulders, one of the hands is rough and masculine, the other soft and feminine. This is Rembrandt's way of saying yes, the father is a symbol of God's welcoming love, but God should not be seen only as *paternal*. He is *maternal* in his love as well. As the prophet Isaiah declared, "As a mother comforts her children, so I comfort you." This is a powerful reminder that God transcends gender. He combines the best of both masculinity and femininity, but he is also in his nature beyond these earth-bound binaries. He is the father and the mother we've all been waiting for, but he is so much more than that. Rembrandt saw this.

But he saw something else too – something that the art critics and the bible scholars have neglected. In the top left corner of the painting there is the pale, faded, almost spectral image of a woman. She is the same age as the father who is welcoming his lost boy home. She looks on with tender eyes. She is a ghostly figure, almost an apparition. From the point of view of the story, she is not a servant (as some surmise) but the boy's mother. And she is a ghost.

Rembrandt's genius consisted of this, that he asked the obvious question that no one else seems to ask when they read the parable in Luke 15. He asked, "Why, if these two sons have such a perfect and loving father, do they both give him such a hard time? Why does the younger son insult him and run away? Why does the older son complain out of such jealously and resentment?" In short, put in the most glaring way, "Why do these two sons behave like they're raging orphans when their dad is still alive?"

Rembrandt, I think, had the answer.

They are responding from a place of great pain.

They are grief-stricken about the passing of their mother.

They are raging about their loss.

That's why they're both so intent on hoarding.

The greatness of the father in Luke 15 consists at least in part in this, that he was a man of great *discernment*, and that he saw that the behaviour of his two sons – in which both broke their father's rules – was a matter more of trauma than of tantrums.

Sometimes as dads, in reasserting the rules and rebuilding the borders, we will need to discern what's really going on when a child rebels against our love. Is this a tantrum that needs to be challenged (primarily through the withdrawal of privileges)? Or is it a trauma that needs to be healed?

The son's disobedience in Luke 15 was terrible, but the father responded with discernment. Had it been a tantrum, he would have said a straight no. But this was trauma, so he allowed his boy to have what he wanted so that one day he might come to realise what it was he really needed – his father's love.

THE DRILL SERGEANT

When it comes to the skill of setting rules and boundaries, we need to learn from the fathers I've mentioned in this chapter and be careful to exercise wisdom, understanding, and discernment. Yes, we need to embrace authority as well as affection in our fathering style, but we must also be careful to avoid two extremes. One of these extremes is the authoritarian father. When I say that R is for Rules, I'm talking about the healthy use of loving authority, not the unhealthy use of toxic authoritarianism. At all costs, we need to avoid turning into what is sometimes known as the Drill Sergeant.

Drill Sergeants control rather than empower their children. They set unreasonable rules and establish restrictive boundaries. They bark out their orders. They expect their children to do exactly what they say without delay. When these orders are disobeyed, the Drill Sergeant father punishes his children with verbal castigation and physical assaults. Such fathers rule with a rod of iron, creating an atmosphere of fear. Their favourite word is "no!"

What happens to children who are brought up by Drill Sergeants? One of two things. The first typical response of a child with this kind of father is *timid conformity*. Having been used to coercion and control, the child becomes a doormat. This is their normal as they progressed from childhood to adolescence. Subconsciously, they recreate this normal when they transition from adolescence to adulthood. They become weak and submissive in the company of authority figures. They never resist and they always comply. When the demands made on them at home or at work are unreasonable, they do not protest. They acquiesce and, in the process, allow history to repeat itself. It doesn't need me to say that this is an unhealthy way to live.

The second typical response of someone brought up by a Drill

Sergeant dad is the exact opposite. It's *livid resistance*. Instead of accepting this kind of coercion and control as their normal, they write it off as abnormal. Instead of letting authority figures walk all over them, the grown-up kids of authoritarian fathers become rebels. Angry at the injustice of their childhood oppression, they become non-conformists, not conformists. They reject the authority of schoolteachers and police officers, employers, and leaders. It doesn't need me to say that this is an unhealthy way to live too.

The Drill Sergeant is therefore one extreme. At the other end is the Concierge Father. He is equally dangerous.

THE HOTEL CONCIERGE

I wonder if you've seen the film *Pretty Woman*. It's a romantic drama starring Richard Gere as a businessman called Edward, and Julia Roberts as a sex worker called Vivian. I'm not going to dwell on the fairy-tale romance between them. Instead, I'm going to focus on the hotel manager, Barney Thompson, played by the wonderful Hector Elizondo. Barney appears at about the 40-minute mark and leaves a lasting impression. More hotel concierge than manager, he is like a father figure to "Miss Vivian" as he calls her.

Right from the start, Barney treats Miss Vivian with respect. He refers to her as "that lady". When he cannot find out who she is from reception, he escorts Vivian into his office where he asks for her name, and for the nature of her relationship with Edward. To protect her shame, he pretends that she is Edward's niece. His only advice to her is to dress appropriately in the hotel so she doesn't draw attention to herself, or to Edward. She complains that she has tried to buy some better clothes, but the snooty women who run the shops on Rodeo Drive won't help her. It is at this point that Barney really begins to act as a top-quality concierge.

Barney calls Bridget at Women's Clothing and informs her that

Miss Vivian is a special guest. She is to help Miss Vivian in any way she can, making sure that she's given the best dress and shoes for the dinner she is supposed to have with Edward and some of his business guests that evening. Bridget obliges.

When Vivian returns from her shopping, she finds Barney and tells him that she doesn't know the etiquette for a posh dinner. He takes her into the restaurant and guides her through the utensils – from the shrimp fork to the salad fork. He teaches her how to use her napkin, where to put her elbows, and about posture.

When she returns from another clothes shopping spree (one of the great power shopping scenes in any movie), she finds Barney to thank him. He replies, "You're welcome sweetie."

He has become a true father figure now.

At the end of the movie, when Vivian needs to go home, Barney hails the hotel limo driver and instructs him to help her. "Please take Miss Vivian anywhere she wishes to go." This is his final act as a concierge. He has provided her with help with her clothes shopping, with her table manners, with her travel requirements. In all of this, he plays one of the kindest men you'll ever see in a film. He is the quintessential father figure. And he is the ultimate concierge.

And it's precisely in the combination of these two roles, hotel concierge and father, that we find a nineties prototype of a 21st century phenomenon – the Concierge Father.

The Concierge Father is the diametrical opposite of the Drill Sergeant. The Concierge Father is the dad who exists to serve his children. He can never do enough for them. His answer to their every request is "yes." When his children need instant gratification, he obliges. He never oppresses them with rules because there are no rules. He never restricts them with moral boundaries because there are none. These kids can say what they want and do what they want.

Guess what happens to children like this when they grow up. They become entitled and whiny, expecting everyone else always to say yes and never no. They protest when their perceived needs are not met. They grow up without proper social skills because they've never had any boundaries. They interpret trivial upsets as traumatic episodes and, in the process, cultivate a wholly unjustified victim mentality. They are easily offended, and they easily offend. They become this way because their father was a provider not a parent.

THE AUTHORITY SPECTRUM

There are two equal and opposite dangers here. The first is the excessive use of authority. This is the Drill Sergeant. He is the authoritarian father who uses coercion and control, which is abuse. The second is the complete non-use of authority. This is the Concierge. He is the father who treats his children like VIP guests in a hotel. He doesn't challenge or reprimand them. His sole responsibility is to say yes to what the child craves. This is child-centric parenting. If the child doesn't get what she or he wants, they see themselves as a victim.

What we are looking at in this chapter is the skill of setting healthy rules. This is a critical aspect of every father's skillset. The Drill Sergeant sets too many rules. The Concierge doesn't set any. The Drill Sergeant exercises authority without affection. The Concierge exercises affection without authority.

The Authority Spectrum

The misuse of rules should not lead to the non-use of rules. Remember Spielberg's movie, *Catch Me if you Can.* When the father (Christopher Walken) catches up with his criminal son (Leonardo di Caprio), he pleads with him saying, "I'm your father." The son cries, "Then tell me to stop. Tell me to stop!" But this is what his dad has never done. He tolerated rule-breaking when his son was a boy. Now he must tolerate lawbreaking when his son is an adult.

THE SOFT PLAY CENTRE

Every father needs to spend time investing in the skill of rule setting. In establishing rules and boundaries, the key thing is to combine loving affection with loving authority. When we watch Atticus Finch on the deck of his house with his daughter, we see loving affection (he has his arm around her) and loving authority (he reasons with her and reaches a compromise with the incentive of a reward). This is great fathering whatever your movie preferences!

If we return to the bull elephants, we can see from the natural kingdom how important it is for young bulls to grow up with a proper sense of boundaries. The older male elephants didn't coerce these younger bulls to obey. They modelled good behaviour themselves and, by gently nudging the young bulls, they pointed them in the right direction. Sons and daughters do not benefit from coercive parenting any more than they benefit from concierge parenting. Neither does them any good either in the short or the long run. Every father needs to work out where the radical middle is for them, but one guiding principle in this book is WWDD - what would Dad do? The Dad we're talking about is the father in Luke 15. His focus was far more on what his son needed than what his son wanted. Atticus respected this principle too. The reward he gave to Scout for her obedience was something she needed – reading books. Make sure that guided reading is something you're doing with your children. The more they read, the wiser they'll be.

Not long ago, I went to the soft play centre with my son and grandson in my local town. My grandson – about eighteen months old at the time – went off to play in a large plastic car. He zoomed around in it until he decided to have a break. He exited his toy vehicle, whereupon a girl of about the same age hopped into the driver's seat. My grandson, seeing this, made to bite her.

My son sprung like a gazelle into action.

Before his son's teeth sank into the poor girl's flesh, he picked him up and carried him to another part of the building. There he stood, far away from prying eyes and ears, holding his boy in his strong arms. He spoke softly to him for several minutes, reminding him of the rules. If he tried to bite someone again, the three of us would have to go home. At no point did my grandson cry. He looked into his dad's eyes and listened to his voice, all the while staying within his daddy's big arms. Resistance, as they say on Star Trek, was futile!

My grandson was released back into the soft play area and once again made to bite the girl. Once again, my son took him far from the madding crowd. He repeated the lesson, never raising his voice or losing his cool. This time, when my grandson returned to the girl, he politely asked whether he could have the car. She nodded.

What a great example of how to set rules and boundaries. Notice the way my son, as a dad, combined loving affection with loving authority. Notice how the rules he set were love-based, not law-based. And notice how this helped with social interaction.

That day, in the soft play centre, a young bull elephant learned what was elephant-like, and what was not.

I'd love to say he got that from me, but he did not.

My son learned it himself.

And I am infinitely prouder of him for that.

QUESTION TIME

Look at the four stages of learning:

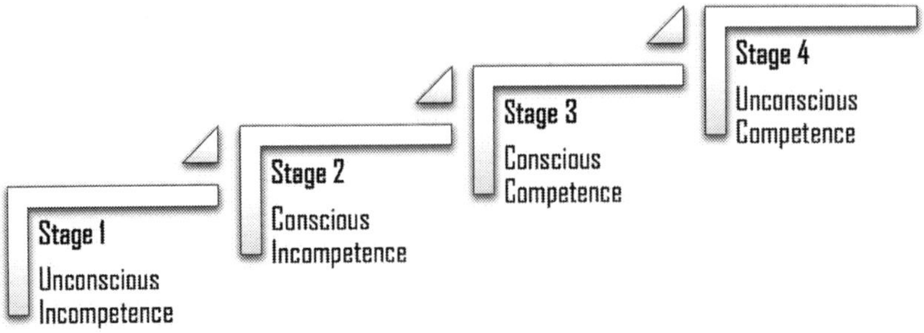

Where are you right now in this specific skill (setting healthy rules)?

How are you going to get to the next stage of competence?

What practical changes are you going to make as a dad in the light of what you've just read?

S IS FOR SECURITY

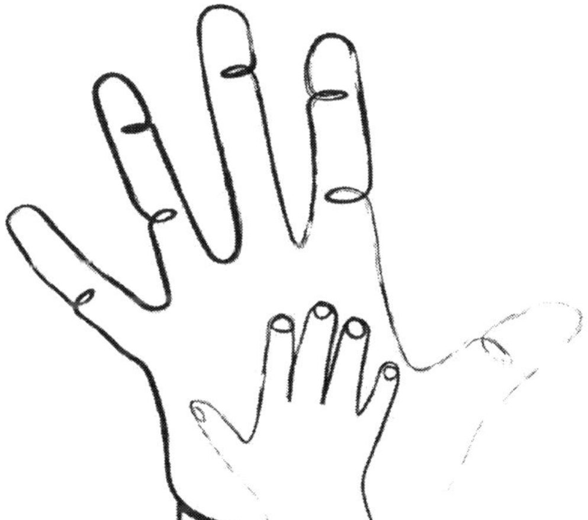

I cannot think of any need in childhood as strong
as the need for a father's protection.

Sigmund Freud

8
S IS FOR SECURITY

We have now reached the end of our exploration of the seven skills every dad needs to master. We have seen that none of us is born a good dad, nor are we gifted with some mystical endowment of fathering. As dads, we all learn to become competent over time by using seven skills. The first is **fun**. Dads learn to exercise the skill of fun and play. We have a unique role in this. The second is **affirmation**. Remember Ben Sira: "A person's honour comes from their father." The third is **time**. Dads learn to invest quality or *kairos* time with their children. The fourth is **hugs**. Dads learn to be a port in every storm. The fifth is **example**. Dads learn to establish the blueprints for loving God, loving others (especially Mum), and loving yourself. The sixth is **rules**. Dads learn to establish love-based boundaries. This just leaves one more skill for us to discuss. Dads learn to foster **security**.

I've emphasized two things throughout this book. Firstly, everything we need to know about highly effective fathering can be found in the sacred Scriptures, especially in the story told in Luke 15. Two thousand years ago, the greatest sage in history, Jesus of Nazareth, told an unforgettable tale about the most extravagantly loving and forgiving dad. That story has stood the test of time. It still gives us infinite fathering wisdom today. Secondly, every skill we learn about effective fathering in that parable – fun, affirmation, time, hugs, example, rules, and now security – has been backed up by recent scientific research, especially within the new and ground-breaking discipline known as the science of fatherhood. Brilliant scientists in the academy, most notably Dr Anna Machin, have used recent neuroscientific research to show us what we've known all along from Scripture – that a father's place in the home is both unique and vital. We have seen this in every chapter of this book as I have deliberately reminded us (a) of what we see the father doing in Luke 15 and (b) what we are learning from scientists like Anna Machin, and from the science of fatherhood.

This is true for our final fathering skill – establishing an atmosphere and connection with your child that is characterised by security. What we're really talking about here is "secure attachment." A father has a special and distinctive role in making sure that he is securely attached to his child or children, and that they in turn are securely attached to him. There are few things more important than this. Ever since the work of British psychologist John Bowlby, we have known that children who have a foundation of secure attachment in their early years grow into adults who (a) have a positive sense of self-worth and significance, and (b) are better able to interact socially because they have a basic sense of trust. Bowlby focused only on mothers. In this chapter, I want to talk about fathers.

SCRIPTURE AND SCIENCE

If we go back to the father in Luke 15, one thing we can say with a fair degree of certainty is that he had spent years building a sense of secure attachment between himself and his two sons. We know this because of the three ways in which he restores a secure attachment with his younger son when he returns from the far country. This father has been watching out for him night and day. In other words, he uses his **eyes**. Secondly, he speaks words of great love, tenderness, and generosity when his son is before him, asking for the robe and the ring, symbols of the fact that he wants his attachment to his son fully restored. In other words, he uses his **voice**. Thirdly, he cannot stop hugging and kissing his boy. He is unashamedly demonstrative in his affection. In other words, he uses physical **touch**. This use of **eyes**, **voice**, and **touch** is not new to him. This is how he has always related to his sons. As we will see in a little while, there are the critical soft fathering skills that are needed to create a secure attachment with your child.

That's Scripture. What about science? Here we need to remember the distinctive function a father has right from the beginning of a child's life. Scientists like Anna Machin have demonstrated that a father and mother have different roles. These are not in competition with each other. The brains of men and women have been hardwired so they respond differently to a new baby. Put in very simple language, the mother gets a kick out of holding her child to console and nurture them. This holding has an **inward** focus. The father, on the other hand, gets a rush out of releasing the child from his embrace to go and play, explore, discover, and so on. This holding has an **outward** focus. The new science of fatherhood has shown that there is no competition here between Dad and Mum. They are a team. Their complimentary brain activity is evidence of divine synchrony.

The way in which this happens is fascinating. In Mum's brain, there is an increase in grey and white matter in the limbic core. This is the feeling centre of the brain – the part of the brain that stimulates Mum into hugging and soothing. In Dad's brain, there is an increase in grey and white matter in the neocortex – that part of the brain that stimulates him to think, reason, plan, prepare.

A dad right from the beginning is primed to turn his child out towards the world. Through secure attachment, he builds the strong foundation for that child to leave and explore, whether that's in the first year when a baby wants to crawl around a sitting room, or at the beginning of the teenage years when the child is about to navigate a whole new landscape that is both frightening as well as exciting. In other words, the dad is primed to be there for the child in their leave-taking and their homecoming. Whether the child is going or returning, the father's secure attachment is critical for that child sense of wellbeing.

Once again, we see how Scripture and science speak in harmony about a father's unique skill in the matter of security - or more specifically, secure attachment. For what is it the father does in Luke 15? He creates the safe base for his son to leave and return, even if that son's story is one of rebellion.

THREE WAYS NOT TO DO IT

At this point, you may be thinking that the concept of secure attachment is still a bit vague, so I'll try to be a bit clearer about what I mean. Perhaps it's best to come at the subject from the opposite direction – in other words, by showing what *insecure* attachment looks like. *Insecure* attachment happens when a dad does not invest in creating that safe and loving space in which a strong connection is established between him and his child. A dad can create *unsafe* or *insecure* attachment in various ways, but three are sadly far too common.

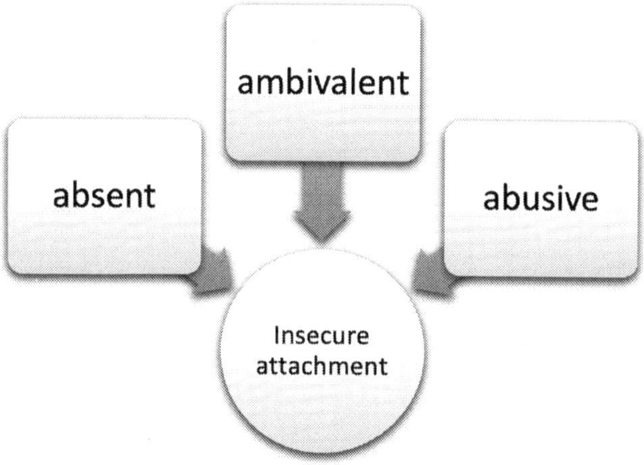

The **absent** father creates a sense of unsafe or insecure attachment either by not being present at all, or by being present physically but absent emotionally. This creates weak foundations and unhealthy blueprints. Children who grow up with an absent father come to expect that their loved ones will also be absent figures in adult life. Their normal in childhood was for their father not to be present. This creates the subconscious template for adult relationships. When they grow up, the children of absent fathers may regard the absenteeism of loved ones as their "normal" too.

The **ambivalent** father creates a sense of unsafe or insecure attachment by being inconsistent and unreliable. Sometimes he is there. Sometimes he is not. The children of ambivalent fathers grow into adults who expect their loved ones will be sometimes present, sometimes absent. Once again, ambivalence has become the "normal". History repeats itself. The tapes replay.

The **abusive** father creates a sense of unsafe or insecure attachment by being the ultimate nightmare. He is the one a child expects to protect them, but it turns out he is there to harm them. The child feels constantly unsafe in this father's presence. This father's abuses can come in various forms:

- Verbal
- Physical
- Sexual
- Emotional
- Psychological
- Religious

The children of abusive fathers grow up expecting this to be their normal in their adult relationships. They spent their childhood in the brace position. This is how they live as adults.

THE CYCLE OF PAIN

I want to be even more specific here about what happens when dads don't exercise the skill of secure attachment. When fathers are absent, ambivalent, or abusive, they create a cycle of pain in their child's soul. Let's look at this cycle.

In stage 1 of the cycle, there is **trauma**. This trauma may be caused by a father's absence, ambivalence, or abuse (or potentially a combination). Lodged in the soul, the pain of this father wound initiates feelings of insecurity.

In stage 2 of the cycle, **lies** begin to infiltrate the soul. The pain of the father wound leads a child to grow up with false beliefs about themselves. These false beliefs are characterised by shame. Remember, shame is different from guilt. Guilt is focused on what I've done. Shame is focused on who I am. As many have said before, "Guilt says, 'I've made a mistake.' Shame says, 'I *am* a mistake'." To say "I am a mistake" is a lie. When a child experiences a father wound, that trauma becomes the door through which these lies begin to seep into the soul. Here are some examples of these lies.

When a child has an absent father, they may say, "If only I was more lovable/likeable, Dad might have been there."

When a child has an ambivalent father, they may say, "If I had been better behaved, better looking, better at sports, Dad might have been there for me more."

When a child has an abusive father, they may say, "If I hadn't been so defective, Dad wouldn't have hurt me."

You see how a child believes lies in the wake of father wounds? These lies become the inner vows they make about themselves every day. They are the clouds under which they live in the present continuous tense of their fatherless lives.

If trauma is to do with the past and lies with the present, the third and final part of the cycle has to do with the future. Here we are referring to **fears**. The child who believes these lies about themselves in the present, expects history to repeat itself in the future. They expect their significant others in adult life to be absent too, or ambivalent, or abusive. And so, the cycle often repeats itself, with the adult experiencing further comparable **trauma**, believing similar **lies**, and living in **fear** of the same sorts of traumas happening in the future. In fact, these expectations can be so strong that they have a kind of self-fulfilling dynamic. The adult victim of childhood father wounds says with Job, "That which I fear has come upon me."

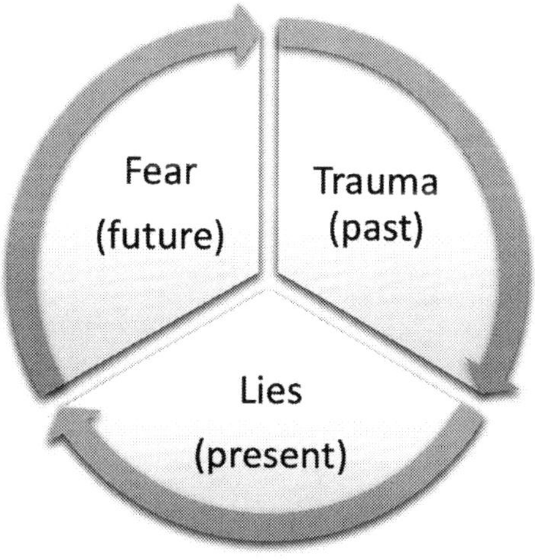

EYES, VOICE, TOUCH

Looking at this cycle of pain, most dads will say, "I want to avoid inflicting this on my child. I want to learn the skill of creating a secure rather than an insecure attachment." If that's you, the next part of this chapter is going to help because here we move from the cycle of pain (the bad news) to the ways in which you can create a safe, strong, and secure connection with your child (the good news).

C.S. Lewis wrote a great book called *The Four Loves.* Being a classical scholar as well as a scholar of English literature, he knew that in the ancient Greek language there were four different words which we often translate "love." Each of these words carries a different nuance or connotation when it comes to that multi-faceted and many-splendored thing called love. Let's look at them.

Firstly, there is ***eros***. This is the word from which we get erotic and eroticism. It will be no surprise to learn that eros is therefore the word used in ancient Greece for sexual love.

Secondly, there is ***agapé***. This is a word that we find a lot in the New Testament. It is self-sacrificial love – the kind of love Jesus talks about when a man lays down his life for his friends.

Thirdly, there is ***phileia***. This is the love shown to each other by friends. It carries the idea of demonstrated affection. Friends hug each other. Some may hold hands.

Fourthly, there is ***storgé***. This is the love that a parent shows for their child. This is the love that holds, soothes, comforts, nurtures, nestles, and caresses.

Of these four loves, the one that in my opinion has received least attention is *storgé*. This is what a dad needs to exhibit when his child is born. One incentive for dads is that his brain releases feel-good and bonding chemicals to help him do that.

How does a dad show this kind of love? By doing three things that we associate with soft parenting skills. He firstly looks adoringly at his child (his **eyes**). He secondly speaks tenderly to his child, telling them that he loves them, he likes them, and that he is especially fond of them (his **voice**). Thirdly, he demonstrates his affection through appropriate, pure, and tender physical contact (his **touch**). These are the three ways a dad expresses his *storgé* love.

If you want a fine example, go to YouTube and type the following into the search engine: Delivery Room/Kinda Deep/ Michael Jnr. There you'll find comedian Michael Jnr showing a video of his daughter just after she was born. She is distraught, crying, and writhing. Dad speaks to her saying "It's okay, baby. I'm right here." His daughter calms down immediately. A few minutes later, a nurse has started work on her and she starts crying again. Dad holds her hand and speaks to her, and she calms down again. He tells her that he loves her. When he says, "I love you," she opens her eyes and looks at him.

This is *storgé* love.

This is a father establishing a secure attachment through his **eyes**, his **voice**, and his **touch**.

As Michael Jnr says, this is how our Heavenly Father love us – his children - too.

THE CYCLE OF RECOVERY

Many dads have father wounds. Having been poorly fathered, we find it hard to father well. Speaking for myself, I have experienced all three types of insecure fathering styles. My biological father was absent. He doesn't even know I exist. My adoptive father was ambivalent. He was there when I was at home, but not there when I was sent away to boarding school. My spiritual father was abusive to me for four years – physically as well as spiritually.

How do we recover when we've been the victim of insecure attachments with our fathers or father figures? Michael Jnr has already given us a clue. In his video, he talks about the way in which our Heavenly Father lavishes us with love. He watches over us and sees us (**eyes**). He speaks words of affirmation over us, telling us that he loves us and that we're the pride of his life (**voice**). He embraces us in his arms of love, reassuring us in our spirits by his Spirit that we are forever the children of God (**touch**). God is the perfect Dad. When we allow him to embrace us, the healing process can begin. Indeed, *secure attachment with our Heavenly Father is the only way we can displace insecure attachment with our earthly fathers.*

Remember King David's words I quoted earlier: "Even though my father and mother abandon me, the Lord will hold me close" (Psalm 27:10). If we experience a father wound – for example, the trauma of abandonment – the Scriptures tell us that our Heavenly Father will *hold* us in his embrace. When this happens, the trauma gets healed. The absence of our earthly father's love is displaced by the presence of our Heavenly Father's love. This in turn leads us to replace lies with truths. Instead of saying that we're a mistake, we believe that we are a masterpiece. Instead of believing we're here by accident, we believe we are here by appointment. Instead of believing we are horrible, we believe we are honoured. All these truths about us are written in the sacred Scriptures. They are not the positive confessions of a self-help guru or a pop psychologist. They are the eternal truths of God the Father. When our father wounds are healed, these truths are written on our hearts by the Holy Spirit, who is the Spirit of Truth. This means that we are no longer fearful of the future. We are expectant. We believe the best is yet to be. We have a strong hope for our future (Jeremiah 29:11). So, the cycle of recovery looks like this.

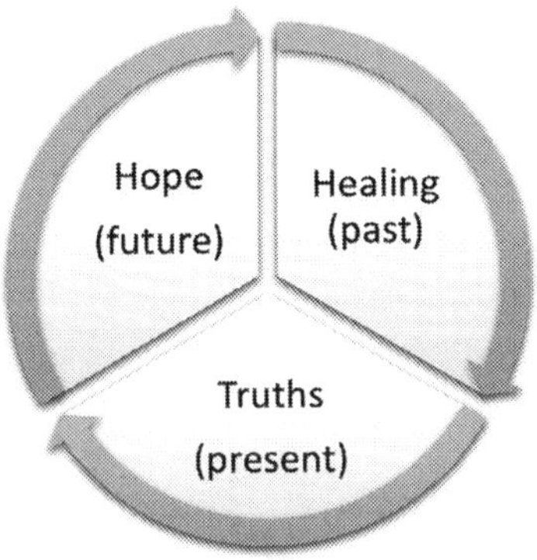

THE POWER OF LOVE

Let me share a bit of my story. I became a Christian in 1977 when I was sixteen years old. I experienced a wonderful sense of being forgiven. The next day I felt truly alive for the first time in my life. I had decided to follow Jesus. I had received a free pardon for all my sins thanks to Christ's self-sacrificial love on the Cross.

However, although I was forgiven, I was not free. The evidence for this was the fact that I loved relating to Jesus, but I couldn't relate to my Heavenly Father. This was due to the wound from my biological father. If he was absent, how could I trust God not to be too? My father wound therefore made me a kind of half-Christian.

Ten years after my conversion, I was now an ordained priest in the Church of England. I was given the task of leading the church youth group by my training vicar. There were only six teenagers. They were rebellious and uncooperative. I therefore decided to take them to an event run by Youth for Christ. If they met with God there, maybe they would be more agreeable during the Sunday night youth meetings – meetings that I dreaded.

As it transpired, it wasn't them that got transformed at the youth event. It was me.

To cut a long story short, I was standing with my six stroppy teenagers when the music group started playing a beautiful song about God being a father who adopts us. I had never heard a hymn or a song on this subject before and I was utterly floored. Tears started pouring down my face. As I felt God's healing embrace, I had an epiphany. 'God is not like my absent biological father. He is my loving adoptive father who will never leave me. I will therefore never be alone because Father God is always beside me.'

I cannot begin to express how different I felt after that. Everything changed, including the youth group! I felt a complete Christian now. Not only did I love Jesus. I loved my Heavenly Father too. Not only did I have the robe around my shoulders (pardon for sin). I had the ring on my finger (my position as a son). That healing embrace transformed me. It became the root system for everything that grew out of my life after that, including many books – even this one.

I share this because I believe that one of the mistakes people make when they have suffered trauma from their father is they think that it's enough just to stand in front of a mirror and replace the lies they've come to believe with their positive counterparts. But this doesn't work. You can't displace a negative experience with positive beliefs. Put another way, you can't displace trauma with truths. You need to experience something as lifechanging and strong as the original trauma. Logic won't heal your wounds. Only love will.

If you're a dad who suffered insecure attachment with your father, understand that a cognitive approach to therapy is not enough. This just changes the way you think (the neocortex). You need God's *affective* therapy. This changes the way you feel (the limbic core). It is the power of God's love you need if you're to recover from your father wounds. This will set you free as a father too!

THINGS MY FATHER TAUGHT ME

If there's one thing that activates and accelerates the therapeutic process more than anything else, it's forgiveness. I'm talking about things we can do from our side, as it were. We can pray for the healing embrace of our Heavenly Father, and I encourage you to do that, but it's his decision when and how he does that. That's on his side. But when it comes to what we can do, what we can take responsibility for actioning, the one thing we should be focusing on is forgiving our fathers and father figures. If they have hurt us, if they have incarcerated us in the prison of insecure attachment, then forgiveness is the key that unlocks our prison cell and sets us free. There is quite literally nothing as powerful as forgiveness when it comes to our therapeutic journey.

If we look again at the cycle of pain, what happens when we forgive our fathers is that the act of forgiving them from our hearts kickstarts the displacement of the pain.

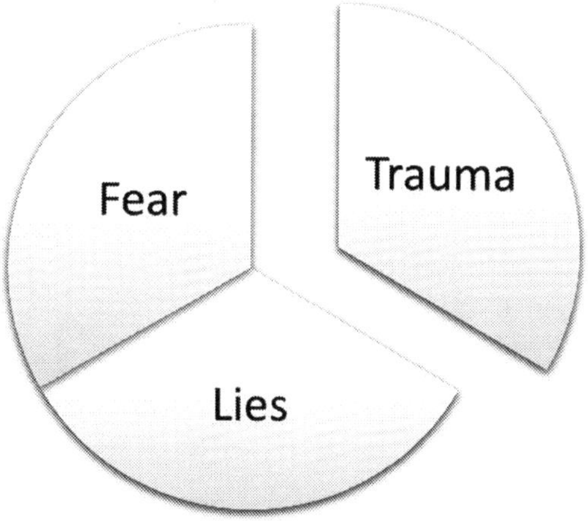

When we forgive our fathers, the cycle of pain becomes disrupted as the trauma starts to get dislodged. In this respect, forgiveness has extraordinary spiritual power.

I have had three fathers: my biological father (absent), my adoptive father (ambivalent), and my spiritual father (abusive). I wrote an article that was published in *The Times* a few years ago, just after my story of being abused by my spiritual father, John Smyth QC, became breaking national news. It was all about what my adoptive dad taught me about the importance of forgiveness. Here it is:

"It was my father, Philip Stibbe, who taught me about forgiveness. Dad had been a prisoner-of-war at the hands of the Japanese in World War Two. For three years, he suffered terrible beatings and all manner of tortures. He never spoke about these things, but he did write about it in his book, *Return Via Rangoon*.

You'd think that someone who had been so badly brutalised would have been bitter. But he wasn't. Dad encouraged us to read a story by Laurens Van der Post called 'The Seed and the Sower,' all about a British officer who, after the war, forgave a condemned Japanese sergeant who had mistreated him. My brother Giles, my sister Claire and I duly read the story and learned the lesson.

'Forgive those who wound you. Don't bear grudges.'

In October of 2016, Cathy Newman of Channel 4 came to see me to share that she knew about the horrific abuse that I and other boys had suffered in the late 1970s and early 1980s in the UK at the hands of the Christian barrister, John Smyth.

When the story came out, I saw my abuser again on TV – heard his voice too, for the first time since 1982. With my wife Cherith's help, I managed to navigate my way through the initial turbulence until I came to a point where I had to ask a question. 'Am I able to forgive this man?'

The answer didn't come quickly. It eventually followed in the wake of another question, one which I have frequently asked over the years.

'What would Dad do?'

And then I had my answer. I knew in my heart that I had to do with this man what Dad had done with those who'd abused him in the war. I knew I had to let go of my resentment because, as Nelson Mandela once said, 'resentment is like drinking poison and hoping that it will kill your enemies.'

Now that John Smyth has died, he will not face justice on this earth; that's something I cannot control. But I can take control of my emotional life and stop judging him. I can release mercy instead. Doing that, I am no longer a POW at the hands of bitterness.

And, like the British officer in 'The Seed and the Sower', I want one day to understand what haunting shadows played upon my abuser's mind, what pain within his soul impelled him to such acts of cruelty. I do not believe in 'motiveless malignancy' as Coleridge called it. To understand is to forgive.

All this I get from Dad – both my earthly father who adopted me and my Heavenly Father who adopted me too. I choose not to live with anger. I choose to forgive my abuser from the heart. By doing these things, we walk out of our own captivity.

I do all this, with faltering steps and a frail heart, because these are the things my father taught me."[29]

As you read this, try to forgive your father for any trauma he has caused in your life. Give him a gift he doesn't deserve. Don't let thoughts of revenge and resentment dominate your thinking any longer. Be motivated by the more hopeful thought that all this is going to help you be a better father to your children.

And please remember, forgiveness doesn't necessarily mean reconciliation. If your father is alive and still toxic, make sure your boundaries are strong. Just because you're now walking in your healing, this doesn't mean he is too.

THE SNOWPLOUGH FATHER

As we come to the end of this book, there is one pitfall that I would like to urge you to avoid. We've all known the perils of what's called *the helicopter parent* for a while now. This is the father or mother who hovers over their child all the time being overly protective rather than simply watchful. Such parents swoop in when a child is trying to explore their world, removing even the faintest hint of difficulty, rescuing them from non-existent challenges. Well, there's a new and even more extreme version of this today - *the Snowplough Father.*

If you want to know what this is, think of a snowplough (*snowplow* if you're a US reader) – those big trucks that turn up on your street and shovel away every obstacle to your progress. That's what a snowplough father does. He looks at the trajectory of your life and seeks to remove every difficulty in your path.

As with other dangerous fathering styles (such as the Concierge), snowplough fathering is a good idea taken to a bad extreme. It's good to be protective. However, it's bad to be overprotective. If you remove everything that's a challenge, you remove opportunities children have of overcoming challenges and learning from failure.

Maybe you've seen the Netflix reconstruction of the college admissions scandal in the USA.[30] It's a terrifying window onto the dangers of snowplough fathering. Dads all over America, desperate for their children to get into top universities, paid for them to gain places through side or back doors by using bribes. Maybe some of them were trying to live their own dreams through their children (that's always a mistake). Whatever the reason, their children – who didn't know their fathers were doing this – have been left with a deep-seated sense of shame. They didn't gain their place through their achievements. They weren't good enough. Daddy's money got them there.

This is, of course, a very dramatic and extreme example of snowplough parenting. You may say, "I haven't bribed anyone to get my child to a certain school or university." That may be so. But have you ever gone to a teacher at your child's school and criticised them for giving them a C minus when you thought they deserved an A? Have you ever gone to the sport's coach when they haven't included your son or daughter in the team and torn a strip off them for not giving your child the place you think he deserves? If you've done things like this – and my experience of talking to friends who are teachers is that this happens all the time these days – then you're engaging in a low-level version of this kind of fathering style, one that may graduate to a higher, more intense, and much more damaging level.

There are two reasons why this kind of parenting should be avoided. Firstly, because it is often driven by fear. When a dad is afraid of their child, or afraid of them being harmed by the world outside, they overcompensate by making life as easy as possible for them, by spoiling them, by going too far on the protection front. This is not natural or wise. The second reason is because if the child becomes used to having everything their own way, they may end up nasty, whiney, entitled, and offensive. In other words, if you act as a snowplough with your child, don't be surprised if they develop the kind of personality that means you may still love them, but you don't like them very much. Letting your child overcome their own obstacles – with your loving eyes, voice, touch available when they need them – creates far more resilient and admirable qualities.

It teaches them to solve problems for themselves, ensuring they develop into mature adults who are confident of their own agency. By ploughing away every obstacle, we may think we are protecting our child, but in real terms we're denying them the possibility of what we earlier called 'black box thinking.'

A FINAL WORD

We have seen in this final chapter how important it is for a father to establish a very strong bond with his children. This strong bond is called "secure attachment." Dads are called to invest in what the ancient Greeks called *storgé* love. This is the love that makes a child feel safe – so safe, in fact, that because of it they grow up with a robust sense of healthy self-worth and a high degree of basic trust in their relationships with others. As a dad, you exercise the skill of secure attachment by constantly using your eyes, your voice, and your touch in a way that is appropriate to the ages of your children. Your children need this throughout all the stages of their lives. It is what even adults need as a port of protection. Even into midlife and old age, we need this safe space as a harbour from which to leave and return.

My father died in 1997 when his three years as a prisoner of war eventually caught up with him. Although he had Parkinson's, it wasn't this dire and debilitating disease that ended his life. It was an obstructed bowel – the awful legacy of three years living on a constant diet of rice as a POW in Rangoon jail.

Dad was now in a coma. When the surgeon said that he could operate and keep him alive for three months – in great discomfort, with no quality of life – or just stop treating him, and let him slip away with dignity, we agreed to let him go. There were many tears. It was an awful dilemma and a dreadful decision.

One a cold January day, I went to visit Dad in hospital. My brother was sitting with him. Dad was not conscious. I held his hand and recited the words of Psalm 23 from memory, then said the Lord's

Prayer, beginning, "Our Father in Heaven."

I felt the faintest squeeze of Dad's hand.

The next day, he left this earth.

That was over 25 years ago.

It still deeply affects me.

Let me tell you why.

There have been times when I have been about to take new, bold steps and take huge risks. On every occasion, as I have prepared to embark and started to explore, I have been gripped by an intense need to speak to my father, to hear the reassuring sound of his voice, to know he is there watching over me, and to feel his hand upon my shoulder. In especially strange and difficult times, I have been almost overpowered by this need for the haven of my father's love. Even when I was away at boarding school, and he in a sense became an ambivalent dad, I still longed for those days when the school term ended, his car pulled up on the drive, and he and Mum took me home. Dad's love was my most secure place. Our home was my safe house.

In the most challenging time of my life, when I was on my own and in shock, I found myself living in my parent's house. They had both died, so it was empty, soon to be sold. I spent my days writing at the old oak dining table in the kitchen. There was a framed photo of Dad on the wall. Black-and-white. His eyes seemed to watch over me while I wrote my way back into a place of emotional health and stability. In the photo, he was smiling. In every photo I have of him, he is smiling. And I bathed in the warmth of it. I could almost hear him speaking to me, saying, "You've got yourself into a bit of a muddle, but you're still a much-treasured son." What relief that brought.

What is this if it is not the afterglow of that secure attachment which he gave me for much of my childhood? What is this if it is not a residue of that same sense of security he so skilfully administered to the three of us – my brother, my twin sister, and me – as we grew up? What is this if it is not the legacy of *storgé* love?

To all dads I say this: invest in the skill of security. Whatever age your child is, use your eyes, voice, and touch to communicate the fact that they are infinitely precious and important to you, and that you'll be there for them in their homecoming just as you were in their leave-taking. Even if, like the prodigal son, their departure is painful and their journey one of rebellion, continue to watch out for them, tell them that you'll always love them, and have your arms opened wide when they return. And when you're long gone from this earth, let them remember your kind eyes, your tender voice, your strong arms, and let this memory be a haven in the storms of life.

QUESTION TIME

Look at the four stages of learning:

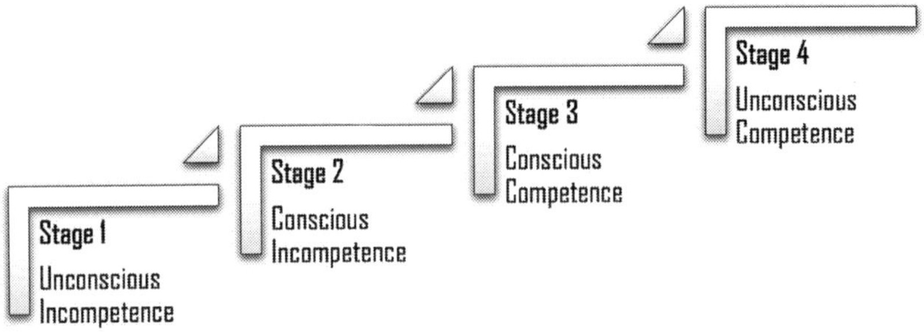

Where are you right now in this specific skill (security)?

How are you going to get to the next stage of competence?

What practical changes are you going to make as a dad in the light of what you've just read?

DAD SCHOOL PROMISES

I promise that from now on I am going to step up to the plate and, with God's help, become a better dad.

I promise to cultivate the seven skills of Dad School, acknowledging that I am a work in progress.

I promise that I am going to have **fun** with my children.

I am going to **affirm** them by telling them how much I love them and how proud I am of them.

I am going to invest quality **time** in them, being emotionally as well as physically present.

I am going to **hug** them.

I am going to set a good **example**, especially in the way I relate to their mother.

I am going to establish healthy **rules** and boundaries.

I am going to make sure that the bond between us is **secure** and strong.

With the help of my perfect Father, I will keep these promises.

And I pray that I will start a chain reaction of blessings for future generations.

ENDNOTES

ENDNOTES

1. I am indebted to Jim Collins's classic book, *Good to Great*, chapter 4 ('Facts over Fantasy'), for this insight. He talks there about what he calls 'The Stockdale Paradox'.

2. While I do not believe that a person is born a great dad, that doesn't mean a person who becomes a father isn't hard-wired to become a great dad. I wasn't born a great dad, but changes occurred to my brain (as they do to every new dad's brain) that meant that I was primed to adapt to my new role.

3. I am not going to spend time proving that Jesus of Nazareth is a real historical figure. As I have said many times in my life, there is more historical evidence for the existence of Jesus Christ than there is for the existence of Julius Caesar. Yet, no one questions Caesar's historicity. I wonder why that is. It's because Julius Caesar doesn't make any kind of a demand on our lives. Jesus does. When I say that Jesus told the parable of the loving father in Luke 15, I am saying that the following have a high degree of historical certainty: (1) that Jesus of Nazareth told this story; (2) that this story has been remembered accurately (remember, the New Testament

era was an oral more than a text-based culture, one where the art of memory was mastered by even the most uneducated of storytellers; (3) that Jesus had a unique consciousness that God was and is Abba (a Hebrew word some translate as 'Daddy') and that the parable he told about the outrageously loving dad is really a window onto his divine Father's heart.

4. For a good introduction to Dr Machin's work, see YouTube: 'Becoming Dad: The Science of Fatherhood with Dr Anna Machin.'

5. Although it isn't known who invented this four-staged model, it is accepted that it was first referred to by Martin M. Broadwell in February 1969. He called it "the four stages of teaching."

6. See Matthew 7:11: "If you, then, though you are evil, know how to give good gifts to your children, how much more will your Father in heaven give good gifts to those who ask him!"

7. For a great Ted Talk in which Matthew Syed explains his theory, go to YouTube and search for 'Why you should have your own black box/Matthew Syed.'

8. For an analysis of the demise of fatherhood in the 20th century, see BBC Four's three-part series, 'A Century of Fatherhood.'

9. See the article 'Playtime with Dad may improve Children's Self-Control' on the University of Cambridge website.

10. See www.storybookdads.org.uk

11. Quoted in the Guardian article, 'Physical Play with Fathers may help Children Control emotion, says study.' Written by Sally Weale. June 30th, 2020. She cites the Lego Foundation at the end.

12. See the article by Georgina Fuller, "We need a Black Dads' Movement: the fathers changing the conversation." The Guardian, 26th January 2019.

13. Ben Sira was a second century (BCE) Hellenistic Jewish sage who established a school in Alexandra, Egypt. He wrote *The Book of Ecclesiasticus* in Hebrew.

14. To my knowledge, it was John Bradshaw who first made this vital distinction in his pioneering and classic book, *Healing the Shame that Binds You* (Health Communications, 1991).

15. The phrase "worthy of love and belonging" is used by Brené Brown in her book, *Daring Greatly*. See also her Ted Talk on YouTube: "The Power of Vulnerability." There she says, "You are imperfect, you are wired for struggle, but you are worthy of love and belonging."

16. See Brannan Manning, *The Furious Longing of God*. (David Cook, 2009), and the chapter entitled 'Healing.'

17. See YouTube, '2 Things Every Son Needs from his Dad', John Eldredge.

18. See 'What was lockdown like for dads?' Article and study on the website of the Fatherhood Institute.

19. For the photographic evidence of Prince Harry and his father enjoying physical affection, go to YouTube - 'Prince Harry claimed King Charles didn't hug him - Here's 7 times he has.'

20. See the article, 'Dads stop hugging their children by the time they turn 10 years old,' by Nathan Lee on the www.londoneconomic.com website. Dr Simon Thompson, Psychologist

and Neuroscientist, said: "We are familiar and aware of the change that puberty and teenage years can have on our children, and these can frequently impact on our relationship with them." Note the following comments. "It is a part of growing up that makes us all more independent, that often means a clear demonstration of us standing on our own feet, and thus showing less tactile affection. However, the closeness and softness of the hug maintains a strong connection and bond between parents and children. It is perceived as safety and protection by the givers and the receivers."

21. See article in The Guardian, 'Mexican president blames US fentanyl crisis on 'lack of hugs' among families.' 17th March 2023.

22. YouTube, 'Faith of the Fatherless: the Psychology of Atheism (Book Trailer)' for a fascinating brief glimpse at 20th century atheistic philosophers and their father wounds.

23. See YouTube, 'Welcome Home: Ruth Graham on her Father's Forgiveness.'

24. Go to the National Library of Medicine website and search for, 'Impact of fathers on risky sexual behaviour in daughters: a genetically and environmentally controlled sibling study.'

25. See 'Stephen Spielberg has Lost his Father,' Vanity Fair online (www.vanityfair.com), by Antony Breznican, August 28th 2020. The subtitle of the article is: 'In key ways, Arnold Spielberg [Spielberg's father] inspired movies that inspired the world.' This article, like Susan Lacy's documentary about his life (2017), came out before his latest film, The Fablemans, a semi-autobiographical story in which the film director explores the impact of his childhood on his filmmaking. Spielberg has clearly evolved, grown, and deepened in his understanding of the impact of his broken family background on his films.

26. I am indebted to Father Gordon MacRae for this story. See his online article, 'In the Absence of Fathers.' MacRae was using the findings from an article by Dr Wade Horn entitled, 'Of Elephants and Men' in Fatherhood Today magazine. See also 'The Fatherhood Factor,' an online article on the National Fatherhood Initiative website.

27. The extract can be found on YouTube by typing in the following: 'To Kill a Mockingbird (1962) Lesson #2.'

28. David and Carrie Grant's book, *A Very Modern Family*, is published by Piatkus, 2023.

29. 'Things my Father Taught me,' in The Times newspaper, 18th August 2018. The article was published under the heading, 'Father's Lesson in Forgiveness.'

30. Netflix, *Operation Varsity Blues. The College Admissions Scandal*. 2018. This is a re-enacted docudrama starring Matthew Modine as Rick Singer, the grifter who acted as a bridge between rich, snowplough parents and the universities receiving their bribes. In a now famous New York Times article entitled 'How Parents are robbing their children of adulthood' (March 16, 2019), authors Claire Miller and Jonah Bronwich reflected on this scandal as they introduced the term snowplow parent to the American public.

"Helicopter parenting, the practice of hovering anxiously near one's children, monitoring their every activity, is so 20th century. Some affluent mothers and fathers now are more like snowplows: machines chugging ahead, clearing any obstacles in their child's path to success, so they don't have to encounter failure, frustration, or lost opportunities. Taken to its criminal extreme, that means bribing SAT proctors and paying off college coaches to get children into elite colleges - and then going to great lengths to make sure they never face the humiliation of knowing how they got there."

The authors then went on to quote Dr Madeline Levine, a psychologist who has been treating the young adult offspring of these snowplow parents.

"Dr. Levine said she regularly sees college freshmen who have had to come home from Emory or Brown because they don't have the minimal kinds of adult skills that one needs to be in college. One came home because there was a rat in the dorm room. Some didn't like their roommates. Others said it was too much work, and they had never learned independent study skills. One didn't like to eat food with sauce. Her whole life, her parents had helped her avoid sauce, calling friends before going to their houses for dinner. At college, she didn't know how to cope with the cafeteria options — covered in sauce."

The authors conclude with the following thought.

"If children have never faced an obstacle, what happens when they get into the real world? They flounder, said Julie Lythcott-Haims, the former dean of freshmen at Stanford … At Stanford, she said, she saw students rely on their parents to set up play dates with people in their dorm or complain to their child's employers when an internship didn't lead to a job. The root cause, she said, was parents who had never let their children make mistakes or face challenges.

Snowplow parents have it backward, Ms. Lythcott-Haims said. *"The point is to prepare the kid for the road, instead of preparing the road for the kid."*

FURTHER READING

All the following titles, whether fiction or nonfiction, look at the role fathers play in our lives, and what happens when that father or father figure is missing.

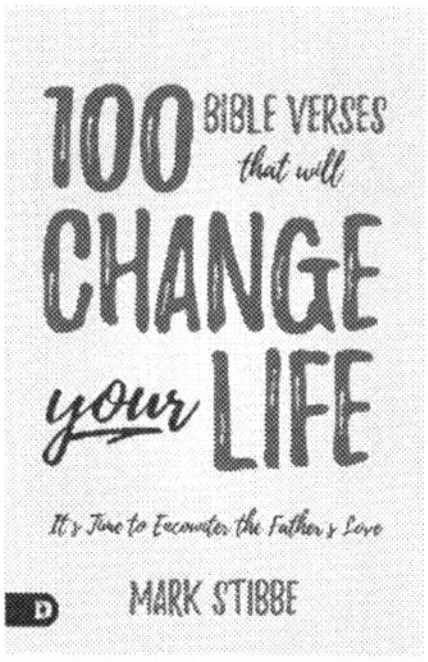

Made in United States
Orlando, FL
25 June 2023

34507995R00109